Jac

A par

Norman Robbins

Samuel French — London
New York - Toronto - Hollywood

CHARACTERS

Demon Discontent
The Rainbow Fairy
Baron Bumble, of Muddlethrough Manor
Jack, Bumble's nephew
Jill, Bumble's niece
Marjory Daw, Bumble's ward
Peter Pumpkin-eater, Bumble's gardener
Dame Dobb
Tommy Tittlemouse, Dame's reluctant beau
Fetch and **Carry**, local layabouts
Demelzia, the Gypsy Queen
Tonio, a gypsy
Antiquita, Keeper of Past Pleasures

Chorus of **Villagers**, **Gypsies**, **Servants**, **Guests**, **Imps**, **Toys**, etc.

SYNOPSIS OF SCENES

ACT I

INTERVAL

ACT II

MUSICAL NUMBERS

ACT I

1	**Song**	Villagers and Marjory
2	**Song**	Peter, Marjory and Villagers
3	**Song and Dance**	Villagers
4	**Song**	Marjory, Peter, Jack, Jill and Villagers
5	**Song**	Fetch and Carry
6	**Dance**	Gardeners
7	**Song**	Marjory and Peter
8	**Song**	Tommy and Children
9	**Song**	Dame and Tommy
10	**Dance**	Gypsies
11	**Song**	Demelzia and Chorus
12	**Dance**	Spirits

ACT II

13	**Song or Dance**	Servants
14	**Song**	Guests
15	**Song**	Peter and Company
16	**Song**	Dame and Tommy
17	**Dance**	The Forgotten Toys
18	**Song**	Peter and Ensemble
19	**Dance**	Rats
20	**Song**	Marjory (Optional)
21	**Song**	Company
22	**Song**	Company (Reprise)

AUTHOR'S NOTES

Jack and Jill was a creation of that great Victorian writer, Edward Leman Blanchard, who wrote thirty-seven of the famous Drury Lane pantomimes, and twenty-eight more for other London theatres. Known as "The Prince of Openings", Blanchard's pantomimes were the most spectacular ever staged, and his final script in 1888, *Babes in the Wood*, introduced the immortal Dan Leno to Drury Lane audiences for the first time.

First performed at Drury Lane in 1854, *Jack and Jill* quickly became a pantomime favourite and continued to draw audiences well into the late twentieth century, with comedians Arthur Askey, Ken Platt, Beryl Reid, and Charlie Chester in leading roles. Like many other once popular subjects, however, modern-day productions are few and far between; professional managements finding it easier to throw together yet another *Cinderella*, *Dick Whittington*, *Jack and the Beanstalk* or *Aladdin*. Small wonder that runs are now shorter than ever before.

Fortunately, amateur societies are far more adventurous, and in recent years I've been delighted by productions of *Little Boy Blue*, *Mary Quite Contrary*, *The House that Jack Built*, and *Ali Baba*; all playing to packed houses and enthusiastic audiences.

So here is my version of an old favourite, complete with two famous set pieces that bring the place down at every performance. Hope you enjoy it.

Norman Robbins

For

Delyth and Andrew Cresswell

Other pantomimes by Norman Robbins published by
Samuel French Ltd:

Aladdin
Ali Baba and the Forty Thieves
Babes in the Wood
Cinderella
Dick Whittington
The Grand Old Duke of York
Hickory Dickory Dock
Humpty Dumpty
Jack and the Beanstalk
Puss in Boots
Red Riding Hood
Rumpelstiltzkin
Sing a Song of Sixpence
The Sleeping Beauty
Snow White
Tom, the Piper's Son
The Wonderful Story of Mother Goose
The White Cat

Plays by Norman Robbins published by
Samuel French Ltd

The Late Mrs Early
Nightmare
Pull The Other One
Slaughterhouse
Tiptoe Through The Tombstones
Tomb With a View
Wedding of the Year

ACT I

The Lair of Demon Discontent

It is a front-cloth lane scene, depicting a vast, cheerless chamber of brooding malignancy in sombre shades

After a short overture, the house CURTAIN *rises and shuddering chords set the atmosphere for the Demon's Lair. Discontent is* C, *bathed in a green follow spot, gazing in delight at a bulbous bottle cupped in both hands. This is almost full of a bright yellow liquid, stoppered by a large cork, and labelled "Essence of Happiness". He is dressed in black and green, heavily bejewelled, wearing a doublet and hose, a short cape, and a skullcap with small red horns. His face is grotesquely made-up, and his eyelids are covered with red sequins. A forked tail hangs behind him*

Demon (*laughing in triumph*) Observe. (*He shows the bottle to the audience*)
Within this simple flask lies all the happiness of Earth.
Contentment ... simple pleasure, and ... what's best of all ...
pure mirth.
For centuries I've gathered it and left there in its place
Each misery and woe that now besets the human race.
(*Smugly*) 'Twas I created traffic jams... Computer faults ...
and 'flu.
Town planners, civil servants and all politicians, too.
In fact, I'm rather proud to say, had it not been for me,
There'd be no income tax at all and car parks would be free.
(*Smirking*) But now at last, my task is done. It's time to ease
the throttle.
No happiness remains on Earth. It's all inside this bottle. (*He
laughs harshly*)

A small Imp hurries in L, *carrying a crystal ball on a velvet cushion. He kneels* L *of the Demon's feet and holds it up*

What's this? (*He peers into the crystal in disbelief*) A
celebration?

People dancing in the street?
The sound of cheerful laughter and the pipe of music sweet?
(*Angrily*) Ridiculous. Impossible. It simply cannot be.
All merriment I've stolen. (*He displays the bottle*) See? It all
belongs to *me*.

The Rainbow Fairy enters R *in a white follow spot. She is dressed, as her name implies, in all the colours of the rainbow*

Fairy (*firmly*) Not so, great Demon Discontent. One kingdom still is free.
Arcadia escaped your net, as plainly you can see.
Its happiness you *cannot* steal. 'Tis foolish to pursue it.
My powers defend that peaceful place. Attempt it and you'll
rue it.

Demon regards her with some amusement

Demon   What's this? The Rainbow Fairy? Ooooh. I'm filled with fear
and dread.
It's been so long since last we met, I fancied you were dead.
(*Dismissively*) Now go away, you foolish fay. Your threats I
greet with scorn.
All happiness in Arcady I'll confiscate before the morn.
(*Gleefully*) Then blanketed with doom and gloom and world-
wide misery...
The earth will be a perfect place for creatures such as me.
Fairy (*sighing*) Oh, dear. You demons never learn. You're so self-satisfied.
Then do your worst ... with my consent. It's time, I think, to
dent your pride.
For though you posture, sneer and mock, you're heading for a
nasty shock.
Demon   With your consent? Don't make me laugh—I don't need your
permission.
(*Proudly*) In ev'ry human heart I live ... a natural condition.
When *Discontent* but rears his head, they'll quickly find all
pleasure's fled.
Fairy (*sweetly*) But not in fair Arcadia. As very soon you'll see.
The people living there are just as happy as can be.
In cottage, farm and manor house, contentedly they dwell,
Protected by the magic I've endued to their old wishing well.
As long as *that* remains in place, it's wiser not to show your
face.
Demon (*sneering*) You think too highly of yourself. I vow to prove you
wrong,

Your pow'rs are weak and timorous, whilst mine are fierce and
strong.

Fairy (*slyly*) Then grant me this ... ere midnight chimes ... if you should
come a cropper...
You'll turn that bottle upside down ... and take away the
stopper.
Allow the happiness inside, to float to earth quite free,
And settle back where it belongs. What say you?

Demon (*glancing at the bottle then smirking*) I agree.

Fairy (*triumphantly*) Then don't let me delay you, for Arcadia awaits.
And witnesses we'll take along, as custom so dictates.
(*She indicates the audience*) This audience shall come with us,
to see that all is fair.
(*To the audience*) If you consent I'll cast a spell and quickly
take you there.

Demon (*scornfully*) Don't waste your time with fools like them. I've given
you my word.
The thought of losing's farcical. Incredible. Absurd.

Fairy (*sweetly*) Yet all the same ... we'll take them for an hour or two of
laughter.
To see you foiled, and all on Earth live happily ever after...

*Fairy waves her wand and there is an instant Black-out. In the darkness,
she exits R*

Demon and Imp exit L

The front-cloth is flown out

SCENE 1

The Village of Serendipity

*A typical pantomime village setting of sixteenth century half-timbered and
thatched cottages against a backdrop of blue skies and distant hills. Cottage
flats mask entrances and exits L and R*

*When the scene begins, it is a bright, sunny day and the Villagers are singing
and dancing on the village green, led by Marjory Daw, the Baron's Ward.
She is very pretty and dressed in similar fashion to the village girls, but of
much better quality*

Song 1: Villagers and Marjory

At the end of the song, Peter Pumpkin-eater enters UL *and moves* DC *to join Marjory. He is a handsome youth, wearing a Robin Hood hat with a pheasant feather for decoration, crisp white shirt, leather jerkin, and boots. The villagers move back and gather in small groups, chatting excitedly and silently*

Peter (*amusedly*) What's going on? I could hear you all singing at the other end of the village.

Marjory (*amazed*) Haven't you *heard*? Oh, Peter. It's the most *wonderful* news. The Baron's nephew and niece are coming to stay with us at Muddlethrough Manor and they'll be arriving any time *now*.

Peter (*dismayed*) Not Jack and Jill again?

Marjory (*laughing*) Well, of *course*, Jack and Jill. They're the only nephew and niece he has.

Peter (*rolling his eyes*) Thank goodness for *that*. If there were any more like *those* two around, I'd hand in my notice this minute.

Marjory (*chiding*) Don't be such a *misery*. They're the sweetest children in the world and everyone in the village loves them.

Peter (*wryly*) Everyone in the village doesn't have to keep an *eye* on them. (*He groans*) They're always into mischief, Marjory. I remember the *last* time they came...

Marjory (*interrupting*) But that was five years ago. And they're bound to have calmed down a little. I'm sure we'll hardly *recognize* them. (*Happily*) Oh, Peter. We could even invite them to the Betrothal Ball.

Peter Providing the Baron agrees we can marry.

Marjory Well, of course he will. *You're* his head gardener, and *I'm* his favourite ward. He'll be absolutely delighted.

Peter I certainly hope so. You're the only reason I've stayed in Arcadia instead of going off to seek my fortune. I can hardly save a penny on the wages I earn, and once I've paid for the wedding ring, I'll have nothing left to keep you comfortable and buy a house.

Marjory (*laughing*) Then make me one of a pumpkin shell, and there you'll keep me *very* well.

Peter (*delightedly*) Oh, Marjory. I couldn't ask for anyone more lovely than you are.

Marjory (*pertly*) I should hope not, indeed.

Song 2: Peter, Marjory and Villagers

At the end of the song, Peter and Marjory exit R *... arm in arm*

Villagers exit L *and* R. *As they do so, Dame Dobb enters* UL. *Seeing the audience, she moves* DC *to chat to them*

Dame (*brightly*) Hallo, boys and girls. Dobb's the name. *Putrescence* Dobb. Spinster of this parish. (*She simpers*) Unusual name, isn't it? Putrescence. I think I must have been named after some sort of perfume. (*She preens*) Anyway… You'll never guess where I've been. I've been trying dresses on in [local dress shop]. Mind you… it hasn't done me any good. The only one I liked was a golfing dress, and I couldn't buy that because every time I bent over in it my niblicks fell out. (*She sighs deeply*) Ohhh, but won't I be glad when this week's over? Well… I moved into my new cottage last month, and it's right next to the railway line, you see. Talk about *noisy*. There's trains rushing up and down twenty-four hours a day. "Here", I said to the feller in [local estate agents], "I'll never get to sleep with all that racket going on. Haven't you anywhere a bit quieter?" "Not to worry, Dame Dobb", he said, "after a few weeks, you won't even notice it". Well… I hope he's right. It's costing me a fortune in bed and breakfast at the [local hotel] till the time's up. (*She brightens*) Mind you… I'm used to not sleeping much. I was a nurse at [local hospital] once. If anybody was at Death's door, it was always me who pulled 'em through. Mind you … we had some very funny patients. Talk about *saucy*. One feller kept trying to kiss me. *Five times* he tried it on, but I soon put *him* straight. "Listen, mate", I said, "You might get away with that sort of thing in a *private* hospital, but this is National Health, this is … and you're getting no kisses from *me*. Besides… I'm not even sure we should be in the same *bed*." And then there's the *casualties*. You know … the ones that come in off the street. The doctor spent *ages* examining one feller, then he pulled me on one side and said "Listen, Nurse. I've checked him from top to toe and I can't tell *what* his problem is. I think it must be the drink". "Well, I shouldn't worry about it", I said, "I'll tell him to come back when you're sober".

Baron Bumble, enters UL. He is an elderly man, slightly vague, but cheerful and kind. He sees Dame Dobb and reacts

Baron (*beaming*) Ah. Dame Dobb. The very person. (*He hurries down to her*)
Dame (*to the audience*) Oh, I say… It's Baron Bumble. The local landowner. (*She pretends not to see him and tidies herself up*)
Baron Where on earth have you been hiding yourself? I haven't seen you since the Christmas party at Muddlethrough Manor.
Dame (*tightly*) I'm not surprised. (*She glares at him*) I'm not on speaking term with *you*.
Baron (*blinking*) Eh? Why ever not?
Dame (*accusingly*) You told me we'd be having succulent slices of turkey breast for supper, and all *I* got was a bit of old gristle like shoe leather.
Baron Well, why didn't you ask the Chef to change it for you?

Dame (*indignantly*) I *did*. I said, "You can take *this* rubbish back and bring me something I can get my teeth into".

Baron And what did he bring you?

Dame (*tightly*) A glass of water and a Steradent tablet.

Baron (*unhappily*) Oh, dear. So I don't suppose you'll be interested in the job I was going to offer you?

Dame (*frowning*) What job?

Baron Well ... as you've probably heard ... Jack and Jill are coming to visit me and I was rather hoping that *you'd* like to look after them. They can't *wait* to see you again.

Dame (*flattered*) Oh. I can't think why. (*She preens herself*)

Baron It's that funny old painting you have in your cottage. You know ... the one of the man with the flat head and the cauliflower ear. (*He beams*) Oh, it does make them laugh. (*He chuckles innocently*)

Dame (*indignantly*) For your inflammation, that feller happens to be my late husband. He was a *hero*, that man was.

Baron (*kindly*) Don't be silly. You're not *that* bad.

Dame (*glowering at him*) Saved hundreds of lives down a coal mine, he did.

Baron (*impressed*) Really?

Dame There he was ... digging along happily ... when all of a sudden the roof started collapsing and quick as a flash he was underneath it ... resting the whole lot on top of his helmet so everybody else could escape. (*Firmly*) And that's how he ended up with his head being flat.

Baron Good heavens. (*Curiously*) And how did he get the cauliflower ear?

Dame (*shrugging*) The hammer slipped when they were wedging him into place.

Baron (*after a reaction*) Oh, well... If *you* don't want to look after the children, I'd better ask someone else. (*He begins to turn away*)

Dame Hang on a minute. Hang on. I haven't made my mind up yet.

Baron But they'll be here in another few minutes.

Dame (*deciding*) Oh, all right, then. But they'd better *behave* themselves. The last time they were here they really upset Tommy Tittlemouse. He was down on the riverbank ... doing a spot of fishing ... all nice and peaceful ... when *they* decided to turn up and keep him company. He didn't catch a thing for the rest of the day.

Baron But why didn't he tell them that fish go away when people make a noise?

Dame They didn't make a noise. They ate all his *maggots*. (*Briskly*) Anyway ... if I'm going to be looking after those two, I don't want 'em seeing me in *these* old things. I'll just pop back to my cottage and change into something more comfortable. I think I'd better wear my battleship dress.

Baron (*blankly*) Battleship dress?

Dame Yes. Top deck cleared for action.

Dame hoists her bust and exits DR

Baron (*dazed*) Right. And I'll go down to the bus station and meet the coach. (*He beams*) Oh, it will be nice to see the children again.

Baron exits DL

Villagers enter excitedly UL *and* UR

Song and Dance 3: Villagers

At the end of the song, Villagers hurry off DL

Jack's head appears from behind the masking flat UR, *grinning mischievously. Seeing no-one around, he enters, turning to beckon Jill who follows him on. They are both eight years old, bright and lively, and wear colourful "Nursery Rhyme" costumes. They move* DC

Jack (*delightedly*) Wait till they find out we're missing.
Jill (*impishly*) And when they see the note we left them. (*She giggles*)
Jack (*anxiously*) You're sure they'll think it's written in blood?
Jill (*firmly*) Of course they will. I've written it in my best red crayon. (*She quotes dramatically*) You'll never see Jack and Jill again unless you leave two pounds on the sweetshop windowledge before closing time today. Signed... Nasty Nigel and Horrible Harry. In brackets. Our kidnappers.

They both giggle excitedly

Jack (*awed*) Two whole pounds. It's the best idea we've ever had.
Jill (*gleefully*) We'll buy Jelly Babies and Liquorice All-sorts.
Jack (*delightedly*) Humbugs and Treacle Toffee.
Jill (*voice rising*) Fruit pastilles and marshmallows.
Jack (*loudly*) And lots and lots of...
Jill } (*together. Almost screaming*) Candyfloss!
Jack }

They giggle delightedly then Jill sobers

Jill (*concerned*) But what if they *don't* pay the ransom?
Jack (*puzzled*) Of course they will.
Jill Not if they're *glad* we've been kidnapped. The last time we were here, we caused an *awful* lot of trouble.
Jack But that was *years* ago. They'll have forgotten all about it by *this* time. (*Brashly*) And besides ... they ought to be really pleased we've decided to

come back again. We're like a breath of fresh air, we are. Nothing exciting ever happens in *this* village.

Jill That's true. It's not a bit like home. But never mind. We've got lots of new tricks to play on everybody and *that'll* liven it up a bit.

Jack (*grinning*) Yes, but in the meantime we'd better find somewhere to hide before anyone sees us and gives the game away. Come on. We'll go down that way. (*He indicates* DR)

Jack and Jill scurry off giggling

The Lights dim and Demon appears DL *in a green follow spot, laughing delightedly and clutching his flask of liquid*

Demon   In Arcady I've now arrived to spread dismay and ruin;
And in Old Serendipity there'll soon be trouble brewin'.
Despite that Fairy's boastful words I'll fast achieve my aim
To steal all mortal happiness and to the Earth lay claim.
Already, to some local fool with brain as dull as pewter,
I've sold, for all the cash he had, a broken-down computer.
No Internet he'll find in there. No e-mails to send on.
No CD-ROM or Windows. All its microchips have gone.(*He laughs harshly*)
Imagine how he'll feel when he finds out he's come a cropper.
His joy will fly into my flask... (*smugly*) and I'll replace its stopper.

As Demon rocks with laughter, the Lights go up

Tommy Tittlemouse hurries on UR. *He is a zany character in outlandish clothing and is usually permanently bright and cheerful. At the moment, however, he appears upset and concerned. He looks around hastily, but does not see Demon*

Tommy (*calling anxiously*) I say. I say. Is anybody there? (*He spots the audience and hurries* DC) Oooh, thank goodness I've found you lot. You haven't seen a funny-looking feller with a green face, red eyes and a tail, have you? He sold me a computer two hours ago and I don't know where he's got to.

Demon (*stepping forward gleefully*) Looking for me? (*He prepares to unstopper his flask*)

Tommy (*relieved*) Oh, thank goodness I've found you. It's about that computer you sold me. I paid you five pounds for it.

Demon (*delightedly*) Indeed you did. And now you've found it doesn't work at all. You want to get your money back. (*Harshly*) Well, tough. In vain you crawl.

Tommy (*blankly*) Get my money back? What are you talking about? (*Eagerly*) I want to buy *another*.

Demon (*startled*) What? Don't be ridiculous. You fool. I've swindled you. You lost your cash the first time round. Confess to me … it's true.

Tommy Lost my cash? Don't be daft. I made a *fortune* with it. As soon as I found out it didn't work, I held a raffle for it and sold two hundred tickets at a pound each. (*Delightedly*) That's a hundred and ninety-five pounds profit.

Demon (*savagely*) But didn't the winner complain?

Tommy Well, of course he did. He went absolutely berserk. So I gave him his pound back and now he's happy again.

Demon (*furiously*) Aaaagh. You fool. You idiot. My precious time you've wasted.

(*Grimly*) But never fear. I'll strike again. Success I almost tasted.

Another victim soon I'll find. In treachery I'm skilled.

By hook or crook, I make my vow. This flagon *shall* be filled.

Holding the bottle aloft, Demon exits DL, *laughing harshly*

Tommy gapes after him in bewilderment, then grins

Tommy (*to the audience*) Well, I don't know who *he* is, but if he's trying to cause trouble in this place, he's in for a big surprise. *Nothing* upsets folk here. We're all happy and peaceful and friendly. (*Seriously*) In fact it's just like living in [local unsavoury area]. (*He looks innocent*) No. Really. There isn't another place in the whole wide world I'd rather live in. We don't pay Council Tax, TV licences, water, gas *or* electricity bills. (*He grins*) I told you it was just like [same local unsavoury area]. Mind you… You always like the place where you were born, don't you? Well, *I* do. And I was born in that little house just over there. (*He indicates off*) But I've got to be honest… My mother was very disappointed when I arrived. Oh, yes. Me dad told me about it, later. "What was wrong, then?" I said. "Did she want a girl instead?" "Of course she didn't", he said. "She wanted a divorce." (*He glances round*) But it's a funny little place, isn't it? All cobbled streets, and little thatched cottages. Still … we might look quaint, here … a bit old-fashioned … but we're up to date with all the latest inventions. Do you want to see what I bought yesterday? Down in Argos.

Audience reaction

Hang on a minute and I'll go get it. (*He dashes to the side of the stage and grabs hold of a long cord and returns c ... leaving the end of the cord vanishing into the wings. To the audience proudly*) What do you think to this, eh? (*He pulls on the cord*)

A large mobile phone trundles on to the stage, supported by large wheels

(*Indicating the phone*) A mobile phone. (*He pushes it off at the opposite side*) Here ... but I haven't introduced myself yet, have I? You don't know who I am. Well, my name's Tommy Tittlemouse ... and I'm world-famous in this village. Everybody knows me. They've only to see me coming down the street and they all shout "Whatcha, Tommy" at the top of their voices. (*As he realizes*) Here ... and you lot can do that as well, can't you? (*He frowns*) Well ... you could if you recognized me. (*He brightens*) But I'll tell you what we'll do. Every time I come on, I'll shout "Whatcha, kids", and you can shout "Whatcha, Tommy" as loud as you like. Isn't that a good idea?

Audience response

You don't sound all that sure. (*Forcibly*) I think we'd better have a practice. Well ... we've got to get it right, haven't we? Make it sound as though you're *enjoying* yourselves. There could be critics from the [local newspapers] sitting out there, and we don't want 'em thinking you're a miserable lot. All together, then. (*He calls*) "Whatcha, kids."

Audience response

Well ... it's a *bit* better. But I'm sure you can shout louder than *that*. (*He practises with the audience until satisfied*) That's better. Absolutely smashing. But I'd better be going now, 'cos I'm supposed to be helping Dame Dobb make the Celebration Cake for the Betrothal Ball next week. So I'll see you later. (*He moves to the DR exit*) And don't forget... (*He calls*) Whatcha, kids.

Tommy exits cheerily DR as the audience respond

Fetch and Carry enter UR. They are an odd-matched couple in ill-fitting and threadbare clothing and are the local bailiffs. They move DC

Fetch (*concerned*) Oooh, there's going to be trouble now, Carry. There's going to be trouble now.
Carry (*baffled*) What do you mean? There's going to be trouble. There's never any trouble in *this* place. There's a *fairy spell* protecting us.

Fetch I know. But it hasn't stopped the Baron's niece and nephew from being kidnapped, has it? Something must have gone wrong.

Carry Don't be daft. How can something go wrong when nobody's been near the *well*? We all know what the legend says... (*He quotes*) "Unless this magic water's spilled, no wicked plots can be fulfilled. But if by chance a drop should fall ... alas ... then woe shall come to all". And anyway ... who *are* Nasty Nigel and Horrible Harry? I've never heard of 'em. And where did they come from?

Fetch Perhaps they escaped from *prison*?

Carry (*scornfully*) Don't be daft. Nobody goes to prison in Arcady.

Fetch (*firmly*) My dad did. Him *and* his brother. (*Confidentially*) That's where they invented their *secret code*.

Carry (*curiously*) Secret code? What secret code?

Fetch (*glancing around to make sure no-one overhears*) The one where they could talk to each other at night by tapping messages on the walls.

Carry (*impressed*) Oooh, the crafty things. (*After glancing around*) And did it work?

Fetch Oh, yes. For nearly ten years. But then the Jailor found out about it and moved 'em into separate cells.

Carry (*exasperated*) Ooooh. If brains were gunpowder, you wouldn't have enough to blow your hat off. Thank goodness *I'm* here to look after you. If it hadn't been for me, we wouldn't have stood a chance of getting these jobs. (*Proudly*) Just think... Fetch and Carry... Bailiffs to the Baron. Absolutely marvellous. (*He preens himself*)

Fetch (*unimpressed*) I'd sooner have my *old* job back. I got six weeks holiday, a bonus scheme, free pension scheme, free medical and hospital insurance, a company car, free meals, and twice yearly profit shares.

Carry (*startled*) Blimey. And what were your wages like?

Fetch Don't be daft. After giving me all that lot they couldn't afford *wages*.

Carry (*irately*) Ooooh, I'm wasting my time trying to get sense out of *you*. You're stupid, you are. Absolutely *stupid*.

Fetch (*defensively*) No, I'm not.

Carry (*strongly*) Yes, you *are*. I bet you can't even *add up* properly, can you?

Fetch Course I can. Course I can. Just you test me.

Carry (*grimly*) All right, then. What's three and three?

Fetch Er ... er... (*He hastily counts on his fingers*) Six. (*He looks smug*)

Carry And what's two and seven?

Fetch Er—er... (*He laboriously counts on his fingers*) Nine. (*He beams*)

Carry Just a minute. Just a *minute*. Anybody can count on their *fingers*. Put your hands in your pockets. Go on. Put 'em in your pockets.

Reluctantly, Fetch puts his hands in his pockets

(*Satisfied*) Now then. Without counting on your fingers ... tell me what
five and five are? (*He assumes a superior attitude*)

Fetch (*at a loss*) Er ... er ... (*Turning slightly away from Carry, he fumbles
in his pockets trying to count his fingers through the cloth and grimacingly
adding. The more he wriggles and squirms, the better. Finally he smiles
triumphantly. Brightly*) Eleven.

Carry (*incredulously*) Eleven? Eleven? How can five and five possibly be
eleven?

Fetch pulls his hands out of his pockets and shows them

Fetch (*ticking of the digits on his left hand*) Ten, nine, eight seven, six... (*He
shows his right hand, fingers extended*) and five's eleven.

*Snatching off Fetch's hat, Carry beats him over the head and shoulders
with it, driving him off* DR

Peter, Jack and Jill enter UR, *Peter in the middle, grasping the others
firmly. They move* DC

Peter (*grimly*) Right you little monsters. I think it's time we had a nice quiet
chat together. (*He releases them*)

Jill (*pleading*) Oh, don't be cross, Peter. It was only a joke.

Jack We didn't *really* want everyone to think we'd been kidnapped.

Jill And we won't ever do it again.

Peter (*sternly*) I should think not. You had everyone worried till Marjory
recognized your writing. And there's *red crayon* all over the coach seat.

Jack (*to Jill; disgustedly*) I *said* they'd never believe it was blood.

Peter If *I* were your uncle, I'd send you home again this very minute.

Jill (*downcast*) But we've said we're sorry.

Jack (*contritely*) And we really, really mean it.

Peter (*rolling his eyes*) Don't you always? (*He softens*) Well, now I've found
you, we can call off the search parties and get you up to Muddlethrough
Manor. (*Warningly*) But if there's any more tricks...

Jack ⎫
          (*together*) Oh, there won't be. We promise.
Jill ⎭

Marjory enters DR *and sees them. She registers her delight, turns and
waves off* R *excitedly, then hurries over to join them*

Marjory Jack. Jill. (*She hugs them*) Thank goodness you're safe.

Villagers enter R *and* L

(*Sternly*) But what your uncle's going to say, I can't imagine.

Jack (*contritely*) We were only playing a *game*, Marjory.

Jill (*anxiously*) He won't be *very* cross, will he? And send us home again?

Marjory (*softening*) Well ... he *is* rather fond of you so I don't suppose so.

(*Sternly*) But you'll have to be on your very best behaviour from now on.

Jack ⎫ (*together; eagerly*) Oh, we will be. We will.
Jill ⎭

Marjory (*smiling*) Then in that case, I think everything's going to be fine. So come on. Let's see a big smile on those miserable faces. There's no place for gloom in *this* little village.

Song 4: Marjory, Peter, Jack, Jill and Villagers

At the end of the song, all begin to exit as Lights fade to Black-out for the end of the scene

SCENE 2

A Quiet Street

Lights are dim

Demon enters L, *in a green follow spot, clutching his bottle and scowling*

Demon   Ten thousand curses. Once again my plans have gone awry. Each nasty trick I've played's gone wrong. Folks laugh instead of cry.

(*Musing*) And yet, there has to be a way. (*Groaning*) If only I could *think*.

In *ev'ry* suit of armour, there's an unprotected chink. (*He plunges into thought*)

Fairy enters DR *in a white follow spot*

Fairy   But not in this one, Discontent. Arcadia still remains Protected by its magic well and all the water it contains. Until a drop of *that* is spilled, your plots and schemes stay unfulfilled.

Demon (*eyes gleaming*) Then should some drip and reach the floor As water from the well they draw; It follows ... with the smallest splatter... *Your* poor spell *at once* will *shatter*.

Fairy (*lightly*) True. But in these modern times each house is water metered.
They never use the well at all.
Demon (*furiously*) Oh, curses. (*Plaintively*) I've been cheated.
(*Recovering*) But curb your smirks. The things I want, I've
never failed to get.
That magic water *shall* be spilled before the sun has set.
So preen and simper all you like, my pompous fairy friend...
Despite your sneers, I, Discontent, shall triumph in the end.

Demon exits laughing

Fairy (*to the audience, lightly*) Such grim determination, we really should
applaud.
But nonetheless, without a doubt his threats are best ignored.
I promise you ... no matter *which* ingenious scheme he'll
hatch...
He'll find 'gainst fairy magic that a demon is no match.

Fairy exits R

The Lights return to full as Fetch and Carry enter L. *They are hatless*

Carry (*disgruntled*) What a waste of time *that* was. All over the village
we've been looking for those kids, and *now* we find out it was just a false
alarm.
Fetch (*wincing*) Ooooh. Don't mention alarms to me. The one next door to
where I live goes off every night and I can't sleep a wink for the noise it
makes.
Carry (*in mock amazement*) Well, why didn't you tell me before? I've got
the very thing for you. It'll put you to sleep in no time.
Fetch Eh? (*Eagerly*) What is it? What is it?
Carry Uncle Joe's hat.
Fetch (*blankly*) Uncle Joe's hat?
Carry Yes. My Uncle Joe was an *income tax* collector ... and when he died,
he left it to me in his will.
Fetch (*puzzled*) Well, how's that going to put me to sleep?
Carry You know what the tax people are like. Whatever it is you tell 'em,
they never listen ... and the reason *why* is because they all get issued with
hats like his. Whoever wears one can't hear *anything*. No voices. No
telephones. No bells. Nothing.
Fetch (*catching on*) So all I've got to do is wear Uncle Joe's hat and I won't
hear anything that'll keep me awake.
Carry Exactly.

Fetch (*eagerly*) Ooooh. I can't wait to try it on. Where is it?

Carry (*grinning*) I'll get it for you right now.

Carry quickly moves R *and exits into the wings, returning immediately clutching a battered old hat*

Here we are. (*He displays it*) Uncle Joe's famous soundproof hat.

Fetch (*looking at it doubtfully*) Is that it? It doesn't look very soundproof to me.

Carry Maybe not. But if you just stand still, I'll show you how it works. (*He holds the hat above Fetch's head*) There's two old men sitting in deckchairs... (*he puts the hat on Fetch's head and continues talking silently for a few seconds, then lifts the hat off again and speaks normally*) running out of the water wearing nothing but her birthday suit And one old man turns to the other and says (*he puts the hat on Fetch's head again and mimes speaking, then lifts the hat and carries on as normal*) "But whatever it was, it certainly needed ironing". (*Brightly*) Now then ... could you hear anything I said when you were wearing the hat?

Fetch (*amazed*) I couldn't. You're right, I didn't hear a sound. (*Gleefully*) Ooooh, I can't wait to take it home and get a good night's sleep. (*He holds out his hands for the hat*)

Carry (*pulling the hat back*) Ah—ah—ah... I can't just *give* you this, you know. It's an old family heirloom. If you want this hat you'll have to give me ten pounds for it.

Fetch Ten pounds? But that's all the money I've got. (*He decides*) Oh, all right, then. (*He fumbles in his pocket*) It'll be worth it in the end. (*He hands a ten pound note to Carry, takes the hat and puts it on at once*)

Carry (*pocketing the cash*) Now off you go, and have a good night's rest, and tomorrow morning when you wake up... (*He realizes his error*) Oooooh.

Fetch (*annoyed*) You rotten twister. (*He takes the hat off*) This isn't a soundproof hat at all. I heard everything you said. Give me my money back.

Carry (*defeated*) All right. All right. It was only a joke. (*He gives the money back*) But it's given me an idea how to make some money for *us*. All we have to do is find somebody dafter than you to try the same joke on and we'll be rolling in it.

Fetch (*eagerly*) That's *right*. (*He glances off* L) Here. There's somebody coming now.

Tommy enters L

Tommy (*to the audience*) Whatcha, kids.

Audience response

Oooh, isn't it noisy round here today? Everywhere you go they're digging roads up and crashing and banging. It's giving me a *terrible* headache. I'd give anything for a bit of peace and quiet.

Carry (*beaming and moving to Tommy*) Then *we're* just the fellers you're looking for.

Fetch How'd you like to buy a genuine soundproof *hat*? (*He displays it*)

Tommy (*scornfully*) Give over. There's no such thing.

Carry Yes, there is. And we'll *prove* it to you, won't we, Fetch?

Fetch (*nodding*) Once you've got *this* on your head, you won't hear a dicky bird.

Tommy (*after a slight pause*) All right, then. Show me how it works.

Fetch and Carry quickly arrange themselves so that Tommy is centre of the trio. Fetch holds the hat above Tommy's head and begins to speak. The routine goes as before, but this time Fetch and Carry alternate the removal and replacing of the hat as they ad lib an incomprehensible story to Tommy. The faster this can be done, the better. At the end of the "story" the hat is removed

Carry (*smugly*) So what did you think to *that*, eh?

Tommy (*impressed*) Fantastic. If I wore it all day, I wouldn't hear a thing, would I? How much do you want for it?

Fetch (*eagerly*) Ten pounds each.

Tommy (*startled*) Ten pounds *each*? (*He hesitates briefly*) Oh, all right, then. (*To the audience*) It'll be worth that for a bit of peace and quiet. (*He puts his hand in his pocket then hesitates*) Hang on a minute, though. I know it works with talking ... but will it work with *singing* as well? They don't half play their CDs loudly next door, you know...

Carry (*sconfully*) CDs. You wouldn't hear an *earthquake* if you'd got *that* hat on.

Tommy Wouldn't I?

Fetch Course not. And just to prove it ... we'll have a little bet with you. Before you give us the twenty pounds, *you* put the hat on, and *we'll* sing a song for you at the top of our voices.

Carry And if you can hear one single note of it ... then *we'll* give *you* twenty pounds.

Fetch and Carry exchange winks

Tommy All right, then. Here's my twenty pounds. (*He puts the money on the floor* c)

Fetch And here's ours.

Fetch and Carry each put ten pounds down on top of Tommy's money

Carry Are you ready, then? *(To the Musical Director)* Music, Maestro, please.

Song 5: Fetch and Carry

Tommy takes the hat as Fetch and Carry begin to sing a selected song. The routine goes as before. Every time he puts the hat on, the others, who watch him closely at first, stop singing aloud and mime. The music must also stop. When he removes the hat, music and singing recommence. As the singers gain in confidence, Tommy begins to speed up the action, lifting and lowering the hat at unexpected moments, totally throwing the singers and musicians. The routine quickly becomes an utter shambles, as they try to keep up with each other. The more confusion this causes, the better. When the song ends, Tommy should still be wearing the hat

Fetch *(gasping)* Now isn't that worth twenty pounds?

Tommy does not reply, but stoops, picks up all the money and begins to exit L

Carry *(startled)* Here. What do you think you're doing? That money's ours.
Tommy *(grinning)* Sorry, fellers. I can't hear you while I'm wearing this hat.

Tommy exits quickly

Fetch and Carry howl with fury and chase after him as the scene ends in a rapid fade

SCENE 3

Peter's Pumpkin Patch

A high-walled garden with a central arch, through which can be seen another part of the grounds and a view of ancient Muddlethrough Manor. At the base of the wall, small pumpkin plants can be seen growing. Blossom-laden trees mask entrances L and R, and a garden shed with a practical door is UL. A water butt is beside this. Full lighting

When the scene begins, Gardeners are dancing, holding watering cans, plant pots, etc. ... and tending to their work

Dance 6: Gardeners

At the end of the routine, the Gardeners exit L *and* R

Baron enters through the arch and moves DC

Baron (*anxiously*) Oh dear, oh dear, oh dear. Wherever has she got to? She should have been here *ages* ago.

Dame enters R *in an outrageous costume*

Dame (*apologetically*) Sorry I'm late, Baron ... but it's Old Mother Hubbard. (*She winces*) Ooooooh. She's had a *terrible* accident. She was on her way down to [local butcher's] to buy her poor doggy a bone ... when suddenly a great big steamroller ran straight over her and they had to rush her into [local] hospital.
Baron (*shocked*) Oh, my goodness. The poor woman. I must send some flowers at once. Which ward is she in?
Dame Seven, eight, nine and ten. (*She chortles*)
Baron (*realizing he's been fooled*) Oh. Well. At least you're here now... (*firmly*) and not before time. My chef's gone on strike again and I've no cook for tonight's party. I've just *got* to find a replacement.
Dame (*beaming*) Oh, you needn't worry about *that*. Nobody knows more about cooking than *me*. (*Proudly*) I taught [famous TV chef] all he knows about it. (*Dreamily*) Oooh, you should have seen his first effort. Just done as I like it. Nice and charred on the *outside* and a lovely rosy pink *inside*. (*She licks her lips*)
Baron (*interested*) And what was it?
Dame His thumb.
Baron (*after a reaction*) I'd better call the children. They've been expecting you all morning. Perhaps you could take them to the cinema, or something?
Dame Take 'em to the cinema? You must be joking. The last time I went to the cinema, it was *terrible*. I had to change my seat every few minutes.
Baron (*shocked*) You weren't bothered by strange men, were you?
Dame (*coyly*) Well... Eventually. (*She preens herself*)

Jack and Jill enter L. *Both are marked with flour and carry small plates, each holding a slice of currant cake*

Jack ⎫
          ⎬ (*together; delightedly*) Dame Dobb. Dame Dobb.
Jill ⎭

They hurry towards her

(*Eagerly*) Look what we've made. (*She displays the cake*)
Jack (*excitedly*) Down in the kitchen.
Jill It's a great big cake. With icing and *everything*.
Jack Made just like you showed us the last time we came ... and all done from memory.
Jill (*offering the plate*) You will *try* some, won't you?
Dame Well, of course we will. (*She takes a slice and bites into it*) Mmmmmm. I just *love* currant cake.
Baron (*puzzled*) Currant cake? But there isn't a currant in the house.
Jack Yes, there *is*, Uncle. We found *heaps* of them in the rabbit hutch.

Dame reacts and chokes

Baron (*hastily*) Well, I don't think we'll eat any more just now. Mustn't spoil our lunches, must we? (*He beams*) And don't forget ... we're having a welcoming party in the Great Hall tonight, so there'll be lots to eat there as well.
Dame Yes. Providing everybody keeps out of my way. Anyway ... never mind that. (*To Jack and Jill*) You like animals, don't you? So let's get you washed and brushed, and I'll take you to see the greyhound races down the road. (*She begins to usher them towards the arch* UC)
Baron (*surprised*) I didn't know you liked greyhound racing, Dame Dobb.
Dame (*pausing*) Oh, yes. You can ask anybody. I've been going to the dogs for years.

Dame follows Jack and Jill off

Baron reacts then follows

Peter enters DR, *carrying a watering can, and moves* DC

Peter (*brightly*) Well, that's the last of the seedlings planted. (*He glances round in approval*) And everything in the pumpkin garden looks lovely. With a bit of luck, we'll have the best crop we've ever grown at Muddlethrough Mansion. Just one more canful of water and I'll be finished for the day. (*He crosses to the water butt and puts the can beneath the spout before turning the tap on. Nothing happens. Dismayed*) Oh, no. (*He peers inside the butt and sighs deeply*) Dry as a bone. I'd better try the other one. (*He picks up the can and begins to exit* DR)

Marjory enters L, *looking anxious*

Marjory (*calling*) Peter. (*She hurries to him*)

Peter (*turning to her, surprised*) Marjory. (*He puts the watering can down*)
Marjory Thank goodness I've found you. I've just heard that there's a
Demon in the village trying to cause trouble.
Peter (*laughing*) Then he'll only be wasting his time. As long as the Magic
Well protects us, everyone's perfectly safe. You haven't lived in Arcady
as long as we have, Marjory, but once there were *dozens* of witches and
demons here trying to upset us ... and every one of them was forced to give
up. There's not a thing to worry about, I promise you.
Marjory (*relieved*) Oh, Peter. I was so frightened. I couldn't bear anything
horrible happening to Arcady. It's the most beautiful place on earth.
Peter Yes. And it's going to stay that way. (*Brightly*) Now just let me get
some water for those seedlings I've planted and I'll walk you back to the
house. (*He picks up the watering can*)
Marjory (*glancing around*) It must take an awful lot of it to keep everything
looking so fresh and green.
Peter (*agreeing*) Barrels and barrels. But luckily there's never any shortage.
If there *was*, I don't know *what* we'd do. Carry it all from the river, I
suppose. We certainly couldn't do without it. (*He remembers*) And neither
can those poor seedlings. (*He turns to exit*)
Marjory (*hastily*) Is there anything *I* can do?
Peter (*looking back and smiling*) You can always keep me company.

Song 7: Marjory and Peter

Peter and Marjory exit DR *as the Lights dim and the shed door flies open*

Demon emerges in a green follow spot and moves triumphantly DC

Demon (*laughing*) The answer to my problem's clear. Soon sounds the fatal
knell.
From Peter Pumpkin-eater's mouth I've learned the way to
break the spell.
If ev'ry village tap and stream should suddenly run dry,
Then all in this repulsive place of happiness will die.
No grass, no trees, no flowers, and no endless cups of tea,
Just drifting dunes of endless sand and widespread misery. (*He
laughs*)

Fairy enters DR *in a white follow spot*

Fairy   Alas, you've still a lot to learn. Your powers here will fail.
Despite your schemes and foolish dreams, the Magic Well
shall still prevail.

Demon   You sneer too soon, my fairy friend. Your counsel I reject.
              From Arcady, this very day, all happiness I shall collect.
              Without a doubt it shall be mine, and though you think you're
                  clever,
              Will join the rest within my flask and there remain for ever.

Fairy (*amused*) Poor Discontent. You try so hard. I really have to smile.
              Though villainy may be your aim, you'll miss this target by a
                  mile.
              So for the moment, fare you well. We'll meet again tonight
              When failure crowns your efforts and you kneel to Fairy
                  might.

Fairy exits and the follow spot is extinguished

Demon (*glancing after her*) You underestimate my skills. You'll soon
                  discover that
              More ways than one there are to skin the allegoric cat.
              With nothing more than cunning I shall put you in your place,
              And Discontent, I guarantee, shall rule the human race.

Demon laughs harshly and exits L

The green follow spot is extinguished and the Lights return to normal

Tommy enters UR

Tommy (*to the audience*) Whatcha, kids.

Audience response

Here, you'll never guess what. I've just been down to the river and there's
a real pirate ship just dropped its anchor. (*He nods*) It's a good job they're
friendly, 'cos they don't half look tough. That Captain of theirs has a patch
over one eye *and* a great big hook instead of a hand. Oooh, I thought.
Whatever's happened to *him*? So I said, "Here, shipmate. Why've you got
a hook instead of a hand like everybody else?" "Aha", he said—"I'll tell
yer why, matey. It's becozz I wus chasin' that scurvy Peter Pan round the
old lagoon when this nasty big *crocodile* came sneaking up behind me and
chopped off me hand with his razor sharp teeth. *That's* why I'm wearing
this hook". (*He grimaces*) Oooooh, isn't that terrible, kids? Having a
crocodilliator bite your hand off. (*He grimaces again*) Anyway ... he
didn't seem all that upset, so I asked him why he was wearing an eye-patch,
as well. "Ahaaar", he said, "that's an easy one. I wus sailin' the Seven Seas

and mindin' my own bizzness, when suddenly ... one of them filthy old seagulls came flying over and did a whoopsy right in the middle of my eye. And ever since then, I ain't bin able to see through it." "Just a minute", I said, "just a minute. You can't go blind because a seagull does a whoopsy in your eye." "Not usually", he said, "But it happened on the first day I got this hook".

Some shabbily dressed children enter L *and* R, *looking most unhappy*

Tommy looks at them in surprise

Ooh. It's some of the Old Woman Who Lives in a Shoe's children. (*To them, concerned*) Whatcha, kids. What's all this, then? Sad faces in Arcadia? (*Sternly*) We can't have *that*, you know. What's wrong?
Girl It's the Baron's party. We've all been invited to it.
Tommy Well, of *course* you have. (*Puzzled*) But why should *that* upset you?
Boy We don't want to go.

The others shake their head unhappily

Tommy (*amazed*) Of course you do. Everybody likes the *Baron's* parties. There's paper hats ... jelly and custard ... ice-cream and crisps ... fizzy drinks——
Girl (*breaking in*) Yes ... but we haven't got nice clothes like the rest of them, and everyone will laugh at us.

All sadly nod their agreement

Tommy (*incredulously*) No, they won't. You don't have to have posh clothes to go to a party. All you need is a happy heart and a great big smile that lights up your face. (*He beckons them to come closer*) Now just you listen to me while I put you straight.

Song 8: Tommy and Children

If required, the Adult Chorus may enter during the song and join in the refrain

At the end of the song, all exit cheerily as the Lights fade rapidly to end the scene

SCENE 4

The Foot of the Enchanted Hill

A lane scene. Full lighting. The backdrop is a view of the hill, topped with trees, flowering shrubs and the Old Well

Dame Dobb enters R, *resplendent in a new outfit, but looking shattered*

Dame (*wearily*) Oh, I say ... What a morning *I've* had. I'd just carried the rubbish down to the gate for the dustbin men, and I found they'd already *been*. Ten minutes early, they were, and their lorry was half-way down the street. Well ... I didn't want the stuff left there till *next* week so I ran after 'em shouting "Wait. Wait." Quick as a flash, the driver slammed his brakes on, looked out of the window and said "What is it, love? What's wrong?" "Nothing", I said. "I just want to know if I'm too late for the collection?" "Course not", he said, "jump on." (*She brightens*) Mind you ... he *did* ask me to go out with him. Oh, yes. We went down to [local cafe or restaurant] for a bacon sandwich. There we were ... all lovey dovey and getting real friendly, like, when suddenly the door burst open and three Hell's Angels clomped in ... all black leather, shaved heads and tattoos. Before we could say a word, one of 'em snatched his coffee ... another one grabbed his sandwich ... and the third one took his Yorkie Bar. Well ... he never said a word. Just got to his feet and walked out leaving me all on my own. Ooooh, you should have heard them laughing, "Not much of a man, is he?" said one of 'em. "No", I said. "And he's not much of a driver, either. I've just looked out of the window and he's driven his lorry over three motor bikes".

Marjory enters R, *looking puzzled*

Marjory (*seeing her*) Dame Dobb. Do you know what's happening?
Dame (*startled*) Eh?
Marjory No-one in the village has *water*. All the taps are dry.
Dame (*surprised*) Oh, I say. (*She remembers*) Perhaps it's something to do with the earthquake?
Marjory I didn't know there'd been an earthquake.
Dame Oh, *yes*. Down in [local notorious run-down area] last night. It did five million pounds worth of improvements.
Marjory (*worriedly*) But what are we going to do without water? We can't make cups of tea ... wash our clothes ... or *anything*.
Dame (*breezily*) Oh, I shouldn't worry, love. There's plenty in the river. It's as clean and fresh as a mountain stream. You can fetch some in a bucket.

Marjory (*resignedly*) I suppose so. (*She glances off* R) But it's such a long way to carry it.

Dame Well ... maybe somebody'll give you a lift? (*Sternly*) Hey ... but not on the back of a motorbike. We don't want any more accidents round here.

Marjory (*concerned*) Accidents?

Dame (*surprised*) Hadn't you heard about it? Oh, yes. The vicar was going out on *his*, last week, and some feller asked him for a lift. "No problem", he said, "but it's a bit windy on a motorbike, and I'd hate you to catch a chill, so why don't you put your overcoat on back to front then your chest won't get cold". So that's what he *did* ... and off they went ... seventy miles an hour down the High Street with the feller on the pillion seat warm as toast. Fifteen minutes later, the vicar looked round and there's nobody sitting there. Quick as a flash, he turned his bike round and came back to look for him. And there he was ... lying in the middle of [local street] with a big crowd standing round him. "Oh, my goodness", said the vicar, "He must have fallen off when I went over a pothole. Is the poor chap all right?" "Well", said one of 'em, "he was till we turned his head round the right way".

Peter and a few of the villagers enter L, *all carrying pails*

Peter (*seeing Dame and Marjory*) There's not a drop of water anywhere. I can't understand it. Even the village duck pond's dry. We're just on our way to the river to see if we can find some there.

Dame (*concerned*) I'd better come with you. I'll go and get a bucket from the Manor House.

Peter No need. The Baron's sending Tommy with all the buckets he can find. But in the meantime, we'd better get down to the river and see if it's still flowing. If it's not, then the situation's really serious. (*To villagers*) Come on, everyone.

Peter crosses Dame to escort Marjory off R, *whist villagers cross behind her and follow the pair off*

Dame (*to the audience*) Oh, I say. Whatever's going on? I do hope Tommy hurries up with those buckets. I can't do any cooking without water.

Tommy hurriedly enters L, *carrying two buckets*

Tommy (*to the audience*) Watcha, kids. (*To Dame*) Oh, there you are, Putrescence. (*He hands a bucket to her as he crosses* R) Come on. We've got to catch the others up.

Dame (*glancing into the bucket*) Just a minute. Just a minute. What's this?

Tommy (*pausing*) What do you think it is? It's a bucket. To put your water in.

Dame And how am I supposed to do *that*, then?

Tommy (*puzzled*) Eh?

Dame (*heavily*) I said. ... how am I going to put water in this?

Tommy (*still puzzled*) What's wrong with it?

Dame (*glowering*) I'll *tell* you what's wrong with it.

Song 9: Dame and Tommy

At the end of the song, Tommy grimaces and exits rapidly R. *Dame chases after him brandishing the bucket*

Jack and Jill enter L, *carrying a small pail with a rope handle, and move* C

Jack (*complaining*) Come *on*, Jill. We'll never catch them if you don't hurry up.

Jill (*grumpily*) I don't *want* to catch them up. And we shouldn't be following them anyway. Uncle Barty told us to stay in the garden till everyone came back.

Jack Yes. But after the trouble we caused yesterday, we've got to show them we can be good *sometimes*... (*scowling*) even if it *is* boring.

Jill But it's such a long way to the river. And the sun's so *hot*. (*She pleads*) Can't we have just a *little* rest?

Jack (*sighing*) I suppose so. (*Firmly*) But we *are* going to help with the water. If we only fill *this*. (*He indicates the pail*)

There is a flash and Demon Discontent enters L *in a green follow spot*

The children react in fright

Jill Who are you?

Demon (*reassuringly*) No need to be afraid, my dears. Your guardian angel, I.

With me here to assist you ... why ... success is yours, whate'er you try.

Just tell me what your heart desires and anything you ask

Is yours *at once*, I promise ... for to help you is my task. (*He bows deeply*)

Jack (*suspiciously*) We don't want anything from *you*, (*to Jill*) do we, Jill? We don't speak to strange men. (*He glowers at him*)

Demon (*smoothly*) How very wise. But all the same, my help's at your command.

You're seeking water for that pail ... or so I understand?

Why walk for half a mile or so to where the river flows?
When close at hand's a better source, as ev'rybody knows.
Jill (*wide-eyed*) You mean ... we needn't *go* so far?
Demon   Of course not. (*He indicates*) There atop this hill, within a
charming dell,
The sweetest water found on earth lies deep inside an ancient
well.
Just lower down your little pail, and with the liquid fill it.
(*Aside*) Then with my help, I guarantee, they'll miss their steps
and *spill it*. (*He sniggers*)
Jack (*to Jill*) Do you think we should, Jill?
Jill It'd save us a long walk.
Jack (*uneasily*) I don't know... (*To the audience*) Do *you* think we should
do it, everybody?

Audience reaction

Demon (*annoyed*) Ignore this puling peasantry.
(*To the audience*) Be silent. Hold your breath.
(*To Jack and Jill*) They'd see you toiling dawn to dusk
And work you half to death.
(*Sweetly*) Collect your water from the well:
Let common sense hold sway.
A minute's work, and then you'll find
You've nothing else to do but play.
Jill (*to Jack*) He's *right*. We don't want to waste time when we're on *holiday*.
There's lots of mischief to get up to before we go home again.
Jack (*to Demon*) And you're sure there *is* water in that old well?

Demon nods eagerly

(*To Jill*) Then what are we waiting for? Last up the hill's a sissy.

Jack and Jill rush off R, *shouting excitedly*

Demon (*delighted*) Success at last. Those foolish brats walked straight into
the trap.
The spell they'll break, and Arcady will fall into my waiting
lap.
Oh, what a *genius* I am. My schemes are so sublime.
Let just one drop of water spill and *all the world is mine*.

Demon roars with laughter and exits L *as the Lights fade rapidly to Black-
out*

SCENE 5

The Hilltop and the Magic Well

The backdrop depicts blue sky and clouds above a rocky dell on the hilltop, with bushes, wild flowers and grassy patches sprouting from crevices. The magic well stands UC and is constructed from yellowy-grey stone, topped with a traditional slated cover. A large wooden roller, which can be turned by a metal handle, is fixed between the two uprights supporting the cover, and a rope hangs from the roller and vanishes into the depths of the well. A small notice is affixed to the stonework at the front of the well, but the words are indistinct and weather-worn. Large rocks and bushes disguise entrances and exits L and R

When the scene begins, Gypsies in colourful costumes are gathered, some dancing a lively hora, whilst others weave floral garlands or whittle clothes-pegs

Dance 10: Gypsies

At the end of the routine, one of the gypsy men, Tonio, enters UR

Tonio (*announcing*) Make way for Demelzia, our Gypsy Queen.

The Gypsies at once fall back to the perimeters of the area as Demelzia, the Gypsy Queen enters UR

Gypsies (*cheering loudly*) Hola.

All defer to her as she moves DC

Demelzia (*graciously*) I thank you, my people, and I bring good news. Once again, our dear friend, Baron Bumble, has invited us to join tonight's Betrothal Ball celebration in the grounds of Muddlethrough Manor.
Gypsies (*happily*) Hola.
Demelzia And once again, we must think of a suitable entertainment in return for his kindness.

All agree with murmurs and nods

Crone (*hobbling forward holding up playing cards*) I'll tell their fortunes.
Gypsy Man I'll play violin. (*He mimes playing the violin*)
Girl And I shall dance like a dervish. (*She twirls around, clicking her fingers*)

All react delightedly

Demelzia And what of you, Tonio? What will *you* do?
Tonio (*shrugging*) Throw my knives … juggle with fire … walk on my
hands. All the usual things. (*Slyly*) But more importantly, our Queen, are
we to know what *your* contribution shall be?
Demelzia (*in mock surprise*) My contribution?

Gypsies respond eagerly and draw closer in anticipation

Well… (*She smiles*) I could sing for them, I suppose. One of our gypsy
songs.
Tonio (*pointedly*) But if you do, then make it one of our *favourites*.
Something we'll *know*. I'm tired of tuneless modern songs without a hint
of melody to hum.
Demelzia (*amused*) Dear Tonio … you're so old-fashioned. But all the same,
I may *just* know one you *will* like.

*The Gypsies quickly settle themselves as the Lights dim and Demelzia sings
her song*

Song 11: Demelzia and Chorus

*At the end of the song, the Lights return to normal as Jack and Jill enter
DR, carrying their pail*

Jack (*halting* DR; *in surprise*) Who are *you*?
Demelzia (*kindly*) Demelzia, Queen of the Gypsies. (*She moves towards
them with a smile*) And you must be Jack and Jill.
Jill (*surprised*) That's right. But how did *you* know?
Demelzia Your uncle is one of my oldest friends, and he's told me all about
you. (*Puzzled*) But why are you here on the hilltop? And carrying a pail?
Jack (*proudly*) We're doing a good deed. There's no water anywhere in the
village so *we're* going to help by fetching some from the old well over
there.

The Gypsies react in disbelief

Demelzia (*incredulously*) Don't you know that's forbidden? Has no-one
told you? If a drop of the magic water spills, the ancient spell will be
broken.

Gypsies nod and mutter their agreement

Jack (*frowning*) *Which* ancient spell?
Demelzia The one cast by the Rainbow Fairy to protect Arcadia from all things evil.

Gypsies agree

Jill (*incredulously*) Rainbow *Fairy?*

Jack and Jill glance at each other and giggle

We're not in the nursery *now*, you know.
Jack We've known for *years* that there's no such thing as *fairies.*
Demelzia (*mildly*) All the same ... the law in Arcadia is very clear. No-one dips a pail into *this* particular well. (*She smiles*) But tell the villagers not to worry. *We* shall bring them water from the mountain streams and pools. In the meantime, you must give your promise never to come here again searching for it.
Jill (*after a moment*) Oh, all *right.* We promise. (*To Jack*) Come on, Jack. Back to the village.
Jack (*protesting*) But...
Jill (*sweetly*) We don't want to get into trouble again, *do* we?

Jill tugs on the handle of the pail and exits DR, *followed by a puzzled Jack*

Demelzia (*to the gypsies*) Thank goodness we were here to stop them. But *now* to help the villagers. Quickly. Gather your waterbags and we'll begin our task.

The Gypsies quickly exit L *and* R

Fetch and Carry enter DR

Fetch (*impressed*) Cor ... look at that view. You can see for miles up here.
Carry (*happily*) Yes. And best of all, we don't get lumbered with fetching water from the river because nobody knows where we are. (*He chortles*)
Fetch (*gloomily*) I bet I know *one* feller who does. He knows *everything.*
Carry Don't be daft. Nobody knows everything.
Fetch This feller does. Every week, me and my mates get on a bus and go on a Mystery Trip. Everybody puts a pound into a collecting tin, and whoever guesses where we're heading for gets the lot. *He's* won it ten weeks running.
Carry (*frowning*) It must be a fiddle. What's his name?
Fetch None of us know ... but he's the bald-headed feller who drives the bus.

Carry takes off his hat and slaps Fetch with it

Carry (*replacing his hat*) You get worse, you do. It's a wonder you know
your own *name*.

Fetch (*scornfully*) 'Course I know my own name. It's Monday.

Carry (*incredulously*) Monday? *Monday?* How on earth did you get a daft
name like Monday?

Fetch When I was born, my mum and dad took one look at me and said "I
think we'd better call it a day".

Carry reacts, then slaps him with his hat again

Carry (*replacing his hat*) I don't know why I bother. You haven't the brains
you were born with.

Fetch (*diffidently*) So what? You don't need brains to be a Kung Fu expert.
(*He performs some Kung Fu movements*)

Carry (*incredulously*) Kung Fu expert? *You?*

Fetch Yes. For your information, my *feet* have been officially recognized as
deadly weapons. (*He preens himself*)

Carry I'm not surprised. You haven't changed your socks for ten years.
(*Scornfully*) Don't you Kung Fu *me*, mate. I know all about Kung Fu, I do.
My brother was the best Kung Fu fighter in the world. The edge of his hand
was so tough he could chop a tree in half with just one single blow. (*He
demonstrates a vicious chop*) Banzaaaaaai...

Fetch (*impressed*) Cor.

Carry (*smugly*) If he hadn't joined the Army, he'd have earned a fortune.

Fetch And is he still in the Army?

Carry (*glumly*) No. The first day there, he saluted an officer and killed
himself. (*Briskly*) Anyway ... never mind about *that*. We came up here to
get away from everybody and have a little rest, so let's find a comfy place
to get a suntan.

Fetch We can go round the back of the well. There's plenty of sunny spots
there.

Carry Good idea.

Fetch and Carry exit behind the well

Jill's head appears DR

She looks around, cautiously. Seeing no-one, she enters and calls off DR

Jill It's all right, Jack. There's nobody here.

Jack enters with the pail

(*With satisfaction*) I *told* you they'd go if they thought we'd gone back to the village. Now's our chance to fill the pail. (*She takes hold of the handle*)
Jack (*doubtfully*) I don't know if we should. You know what the gypsy woman told us. It's against the law.
Jill Yes. And she *also* said the well was a *magic* one. If you'll believe *that*, you'll believe anything.
Jack (*brightening*) You're right. And there's no sense in walking miles to the river for water when all we want's right here. Come on. Let's get some.

They hurry to the well. Putting the pail beside the well, Jill peers into its depths whilst Jack winds the handle to raise the well bucket

Jill (*excitedly*) It's coming up. And it's full to the top. Wind faster. Wind faster.

Jack turns the handle faster and at last the well bucket comes into sight

Jack (*panting*) Quick. Fill the pail.

Jill picks up the pail and lowers it into the bucket

Jill (*delightedly*) I've got it. I've got it.

Jack lets go of the handle and dashes to help Jill with the pail. The handle reverses its turn and the well bucket sinks out of sight again. They hoist the pail out of the well in triumph

Jack (*beaming*) Wait till they see *this*.

Fetch and Carry's heads appear from behind the well

Fetch What's going on?
Carry What are *you* doing here?

They emerge and see the pail of water

Fetch (*horrified*) They've used the well. They've touched the water.
Carry (*in a panic*) Get the fire brigade. Call the p'lice.
Fetch (*clutching Carry*) Don't panic. Don't panic.
Carry (*pushing him off and turning to Jack and Jill*) Have you *spilled* any? Did any of it *drip*?
Jill (*annoyed*) Of course it didn't. We haven't lost a drop. Look.
Carry (*to Fetch*) Quick. We've got to get it back into the well.

*Fetch and Carry grab the handle of the pail and attempt to take it away from
Jack and Jill*

Jack (*resisting*) Let go of it. Let go.

*A tug of war develops as they struggle for possession with much shouting and
vigour. At last Fetch and Carry let go and Jack and Jill fall backwards,
causing the bucket to fly over their heads and into the wings with a crash*

(*Sitting up; wailing*) Owwwww. (*He holds his head*)
Jill (*getting up; furiously*) *Now* look what you've done. Just wait till Uncle
Barty hears about it.
Carry (*gazing off* DL; *stunned*) The water. You've spilled the water.
Fetch (*stricken*) What are we going to do?
Carry (*aghast*) We can't do *anything*. It's too late.

*The Lights dim rapidly and a flash announces the arrival of Demon
Discontent in a green follow spot, clutching his flask*

Demon (*gleefully*) How right you are. That precious spell that kept you safe
has gone.
Of all who live in Arcady, their master I, from this day on.
My ev'ry wish, my ev'ry whim, my least suggestion made,
Will be ... without discussion ... by the populace obeyed.
Fetch (*gaping*) Who's *that*?
Carry Sounds like [unpopular Prime Minister].
Demon (*to the audience*) Without a doubt, I've won the game. I'll now do
as I please.
The happiness of Earth is mine. I've brought them to their
knees. (*He laughs harshly*)
Fetch It is [unpopular Prime Minister]. Quick. Let's go warn everybody.

Fetch and Carry hurry off R

Demon (*calling gleefully*) Come, *Jealousy* ... *Deceit* and *Woe*;
Come *Misery* and *Fear*.
Come *Malice*... *Spite*... *Mistrust* and *Lies*...
Your Master bids you *all* appear.

Ragged and grotesque figures, the Spirits enter L *and* R *and form a half-
circle around Demon*

Jill pulls Jack to his feet as he continues to hold his head and sob

> And now, to celebrate my win,
> Let revelry ... at once ... begin;
> Whilst I my precious flask shall fill
> By courtesy of *Jack* and *Jill*.

Demon indicates them, laughs harshly and exits

The Spirits break into a furious dance of victory

Jill helps the injured Jack to exit

Dance 12: Spirits

At the end of the dance they form a triumphant tableau as——

—the Curtain *falls*

ACT II

Scene 1

The Great Hall of Muddlethrough Manor

The interior of the Baron's stately home, with suits of armour, ancestral portraits, etc. on display

When the Curtain *rises, Maids with feather dusters are busily engaged in cleaning, whilst liveried Footmen polish silver trays, etc. All are singing and/ or dancing*

Song or Dance 13: Servants

At the end of the routine, all exit brightly as Tommy enters UR, *dressed in a garishly-coloured evening suit with outsized jacket and too short trousers, violently clashing shirt, bow tie and striped socks. He moves* DC

Tommy (*calling brightly*) Whatcha, kids.

Audience response as he glances round

Blimey. It's a bit quiet round here. I must be the first to arrive. Mind you … I'm not surprised. They've got half the road up outside, trying to find a blocked *drain*. And the Mayor—you know the Mayor, don't you—[local Mayor], well, he's *furious* about it. He came rushing out of the Town Hall shouting "Look at the mess you're making. Mud and tarmac all over the place. Road drills deafening everybody. Rush-hour traffic at a standstill. You ought to be ashamed of yourselves. And you can watch what you're doing with your *Dyno-rod* as well. You've had the Mayoress off the lavatory twice".

Baron enters DL, *looking resplendent in his finery*

Baron (*seeing Tommy and beaming*) Ah, Thomas. You haven't seen Dame Dobb, have you? I want her to send an urgent e-mail to the Employment Agency. One of the waiters hasn't turned up and the guests will be here in a few minutes.

Tommy (*eagerly*) Ooooh. Here. How about if *I* helped to serve?

Baron (*warily*) You? Have you worked with food before?

Tommy Course I have. I worked at [local restaurant] till they sacked me for helping a customer.

Baron (*surprised*) What?

Tommy Well... He'd got a cold, you see, and he sneezed so hard his false teeth shot right across the restaurant and smashed on the opposite wall.

Baron Good heavens.

Tommy Well, he couldn't eat anything *without* 'em, so quick as a flash, I dashed over to his table and said "Don't worry, sir. My brother'll fix you up with a new set in five minutes". And when I got back with 'em they fitted so well, he gave me a ten pound tip.

Baron (*puzzled*) So why did you get the sack?

Tommy I haven't a *clue*. But it happened just after he said he was going to write to the [local newspaper] and tell everybody my brother was the world's best dentist. "No, no", I said, "my brother's not a *dentist*, he's an *undertaker*". Two minutes later I was out in the street.

Baron Well... It sounds like you did your best, so I'll give you a chance. (*Firmly*) But no mistakes. I want tonight to be a night they'll never forget.

Baron exits DL

Tommy (*to the audience*) Oooooh, did you hear that, everybody? I'm going to be a waiter. (*He thinks*) Now what can I do first? (*He beams*) I know. I'll go down to the kitchen and sew great big buttons on to the King Edwards. Well ... *somebody* might want a jacket potato. See you later.

Tommy exits DR

Marjory and Peter enter DL *and move* DC. *Marjory is in a ball gown, and Peter in a clean, but well-worn tunic and shirt*

Peter Oh, Marjory. I'm so nervous. What if the Baron won't let us get married?

Marjory (*surprised*) Of course he will. You're the best gardener he's ever had and after all the water you carried from the river this afternoon, he couldn't possibly refuse.

Peter (*amused*) I didn't do it *alone*, you know. Everyone in the village helped. Not to mention Demelzia and the gypsies.

Marjory (*loyally*) Yes. But you carried the most. And I'll be very much surprised if Uncle Barty doesn't give you a pay rise, too.

Peter (*lightly*) Well, I wouldn't say no to *that*. But if anyone deserves a pay rise it's Dame Dobb. How she found time to do that mouth-watering spread in the Dining Hall *and* keep Jack and Jill out of mischief, I can't imagine.

Marjory (*laughing*) Don't be mean. They've been good as gold all week. And you must admit, they've certainly brightened up the manor-house.
Peter (*drily*) Yes. They never turn the lights off. (*He smiles*) But never mind *them*. Let's find the Baron before anyone else arrives and see what he has to say about me marrying you.

Peter and Marjory exit happily DL

Fetch backs cautiously on to the stage UR *and Carry backs on* UL

With exaggerated steps they move C *and collide. With yells of fright they turn to face each other and Carry snatches off his hat and beats Fetch across the shoulders with it*

Fetch (*trying to protect himself*) Ow. Ow. Ooooh. Ooooh.
Carry (*annoyed*) What were you creeping round like *that* for? I thought I told you to wait outside while I made sure the coast was clear. (*He replaces his hat*)
Fetch (*unhappily*) I know. But I didn't like being out there on me own. Not after what's happened.
Carry (*incredulously*) You're not telling me you were *scared*?

Fetch looks embarrassed

I don't believe it. (*Pityingly*) A grown man like you and you're scared of your own *shadow*. (*Smugly*) When I was *your* age, I didn't know the *meaning* of fear ... and I certainly hadn't a *clue* what panic, timidity or intimidation meant. And do you know why that was?
Fetch Yes. You didn't have a dictionary.
Carry (*sharply*) No, it wasn't. (*Boasting*) It was because I was a high falutin', rootin', tootin', six-gun shootin' *cowboy*. (*He mimes shooting with his index fingers*) K-powwwww. K-powwwww.
Fetch (*scornfully*) Give over.
Carry (*firmly*) Give over, *nothing*. I was the toughest man in [local district] and I'd be cow-punching *now* if the horse I was riding hadn't suddenly gone beserk and nearly killed me. (*With great drama*) There it was ... bucking up and down and jerking from side to side like a mad thing while I tried to hang on ... but I didn't have a chance. Out of the saddle I went, foot caught in the stirrup, head bouncing on the ground and the horse going faster and faster and faster. Then just as I was losing consciousness ... a miracle happened.
Fetch Yes. The manager came out of Tesco's and pulled the plug out. (*He chortles*)

Carry (*peeved*) Har. Har. Very *funny*. (*He pushes him*) Well, just for that, *you* can tell the Baron what happened on top of the magic hill. (*He moves* US *as though to exit*)

Fetch (*dismayed*) Oh, no. (*He hurries after him*) Don't make *me* tell him. You know folks who bring bad news always get the blame. He'll probably give me the sack. Can't somebody else do it?

Carry (*resolutely*) Like *who*, for instance?

Dome Dobb enters DR, *looking very worried*

She does not notice them, but they see her and exchange delighted glances

Dame (*to the audience*) Oh, I *say*. Thank goodness there was nobody else around when Jack and Jill came home. He'd a bump on his head the size of [local hill or monument] and there wasn't a sticking plaster in the place. I had to patch him up with vinegar and brown paper and now he smells like a refugee from a chip shop. (*Tiredly*) He should have seen a *doctor*, really, but you don't know what's best, do you? There's so many medical programmes on the box these days ... *Casualty*, *Holby City*, *ER*, *Peak Practice* [or similar series]. I didn't know whether to take him to a hospital or the television studios. (*Concerned*) But it's the *Baron* I'm worried about. He'll have a heart attack when he finds out what's happened ... and he's already got *one* foot in the grate.

Carry (*tapping her on the shoulder*) You mean the grave. One foot in the grave.

Dame (*turning to him*) No, no. The *grate*. He wants to be cremated. (*She realizes*) Ohhhh. It's *them*. (*She glowers at them angrily*) What are *you* doing here?

Fetch (*moving down*) We've come to warn everybody. Now the spell's broken, there's terrible things happening all over the village.

Carry Yes. Some feller rushed into [local health food shop], took all the money from the till, ate every prune and fig in the place and dashed off again.

Dame (*aghast*) Couldn't anybody catch him?

Fetch No. He'll be on the run for weeks.

Dame (*grimly*) Yes. Well, I blame everything on you two. If you hadn't tried to take that pail off Jack and Jill, none of this would have happened. You're nothing but a pair of incontinents.

Carry You mean *incompetents*. Incontinent is when you can't hold water.

Dame (*pointedly*) Well?

Fetch Anyway ... it wasn't *our* job to keep an eye on 'em. If it's anybody's fault it's *yours*.

Carry (*agreeing*) Yes. And if somebody's got to tell the Baron what's happened, *we* think it should be *you*.

Dame (*indignantly*) I beg your puddin'. I've a good mind to... (*She halts and turns to the audience, a horrified expression on her face*) Oh, I say. They're *right*, aren't they? I *was* supposed to be keeping an eye on 'em. (*Worriedly*) What am I going to do? They'll all blame *me* 'cos the spell's been broken and I'll be kicked out of the country. (*Stricken*) I'll be homeless. Penniless. And nobody'll talk to me... I may as well throw meself off the top of a twenty storey building.

Fetch Don't be daft. There's no twenty storey buildings in this village.

Dame (*faintly*) In that case I'll jump off two ten storey ones.

Dame totters off RC

Carry (*to Fetch; gleefully*) That puts *us* in the clear. Nobody'll blame us *now*. Come on. Let's go celebrate.

Fetch and Carry exit L *delightedly*

Jack and Jill cautiously enter DR, *looking very subdued. Jack's forehead is swathed in wet-looking brown paper*

Jill tiptoes US *to watch Dame go, then returns to Jack*

Jill (*concerned*) Poor Dame Dobb. You don't think she'll *really* jump off a building, do you?

Jack Course not. (*Firmly*) But she mustn't be blamed for what *we* did. We've got to tell everyone the truth.

Jill (*afraid*) Uncle Barty'll be awfully cross with us. He might even throw us into *prison*.

Jack But we didn't *mean* to do it, did we? It was all that horrible demon's fault. If it hadn't been for him, none of this would have happened.

Jill So what are we going to do?

Jack I know. We'll write a letter explaining everything and then run away before they find it.

Jill But where will we go?

Jack Who cares? When they find out it was us who spilled the water and broke the spell, they'll never want to see us again.

Jill You're right. (*Annoyed*) Oooh, I hate that nasty Demon.

Jack (*glancing off* L) Look out. Somebody's coming. Let's go write that letter.

Jack and Jill hurry off DR *as the Guests and Gypsies enter* UL *and* UR, *all in colourful costumes*

Song 14: Guests

At the end of the song, Baron bustles in DL, *beaming happily as he moves* C

Baron Welcome to Muddlethrough Manor, everyone. (*He calls* R) Waiter. Waiter.

Tommy rushes on in an oversized tail-jacket and chef's hat, carrying a large plate and a handkerchief

Guests look on with amusement

Tommy (*to the audience*) Whatcha, kids. (*To Baron*) You called, sir? (*He spits on the plate and vigorously polishes it with the handkerchief*)
Baron (*noticing Tommy's actions*) What are you *doing*?
Tommy Polishing this plate. I'm polishing every plate in the kitchen before folks put their food on 'em. (*He polishes harder*)
Baron (*horrified*) But you're doing it with your *handkerchief*.
Tommy (*reassuringly*) Yes. It's all right, though. It's not a clean one.

As the Baron reacts, Marjory and Peter enter UL, *hand in hand*

Marjory (*moving down to Baron*) Oh, *there* you are, Uncle Barty. We've been looking for you everywhere.
Peter There's something important we want to ask you.

There is a flash, and Demon enters DL, *carrying his flask. The Lights dim and the green follow spot highlights him*

Tommy Blimey. It's [unpopular personage] again.

All gape as Demon advances C

Demon (*hissing*) At last ... the cursed spell that kept you safe in earthly bliss
Is broken, and the time has come to add your happiness to this.
(*He shows the flask*)
From this day on I reign supreme. Your carefree days are spent
So come, greet your new sovereign ... the Demon Discontent.
(*He laughs*)

As everyone reacts, Fairy enters R *in a white follow spot*

Fairy (*firmly*) One moment. Ere you claim your prize, accept this warning clear.
Your cruel trick on Jack and Jill, I guarantee, will cost you dear.

Though with their help the spell you broke, you'll very shortly see

The people of Arcadia can still rely on *me*.

Demon (*triumphantly*) Too late. The victory is mine. Exactly as intended.

Fairy   You crow too soon. Remember this... The day has not yet ended.

If all the water that was spilled is to the well restored

By those who spilled it, then, my friend, *your* plans go overboard.

Demon   And tell me, pray, how that could be? How could those drops be found?

The magic water left the pail and soaked into the thirsty ground.

Fairy (*calmly*) Quite so. But as you're well aware, unknown to humankind,

Beneath the hill a land exists where all that's lost they'd quickly find.

If Jack or Jill descends the well and triumph in their quest

Ere midnight chimes, then mark my words, you'll never come off best.

Demon (*smugly*) You jest, of course? That realm is *mine*. They'd never venture there.

They're children ... weak and fearful and ... in short ... they wouldn't *dare*.

Marjory (*dismayed*) He's right. We couldn't *possibly* let them go down the well.

Peter Perhaps not. But there's nothing to stop *me* going down and finding the water, then letting *them* put it back.

Demon looks furious as everyone else reacts excitedly

Fairy (*to Peter*) Well spoken, Master Peter. Their Champion you shall be.

And Discontent, the folly of his ways will swiftly see.

(*To Demon; sweetly*) So *do* go on collecting, though as time is running short,

I think you'll find on his return, that all your efforts count for naught.

Fairy laughs lightly, exits R and the white follow spot goes out

Demon (*calling after her*) Not so. My imps shall fill the flask.

If not then woe betide 'em.

(*To Peter, savagely*) Those magic drops you'll *never* find

I'll get there *first* and *hide 'em*.

Demon rapidly exits DL *as the green Light goes out and normal level is restored*

All relax

Baron (*weakly*) Ooooh. I feel all discumknockerated. (*Rallying*) What did she mean, Jack and Jill helped to break the spell? (*He glances round irately*) Where *are* they? And where's Dame Dobb?
Peter (*decisively*) Never mind that. We can find out what happened, *later.* Right now I've to go down the magic well and find the missing water.

Guests etc. nod their agreement

Marjory (*anxiously*) Oh, Peter, be careful. You don't know *what* might be down there.
Peter (*bravely*) Don't worry, Marjory. I'll be back before you know it. And once the spell's in place again, I'm sure the Baron will be only too happy to give us permission to marry. Now cheer up and give me a smile to send me on my way. As long as you believe in me, there's nothing in the world going to make me lose heart.

Song 15: Peter and Company

At the end of the song there is a Black-out

SCENE 2

The Foot of the Hill

As Act I, Scene 4. Full Lighting

Jack enters L, *carrying a small fardel on a stick*

Jack (*calling over his shoulder, anxiously*) Hurry up, Jill. We mustn't let anyone see us. (*He crosses* C)

Jill enters , trailing her fardel and protesting

Jill My *legs* are tired.
Jack So are mine, but we can't sit down *here.* I'm sure we're being followed.
Jill (*turning to look off* L) *I* can't see anybody.
Jack Neither can I, but they're bound to have found our letter by now, so everyone in Arcadia will be looking for us.

Jill (*hopefully*) If we said we're sorry again ... really and truly sorry ... do you think they'd forgive us?

Jack (*shaking his head*) No, I don't. That's why we've got to keep running.

Jill (*persisting*) But ... s'pose we could find that nasty old Demon, and make *him* go away?

Jack (*reluctantly*) Well ... they might do *then*. But how would do we *do* it? We're only children and we don't even know where to find him. And besides...

Jill (*glancing off* L) Look out. Someone's coming.

Jack (*indicating* R) Quick. Behind that old milestone.

Jack and Jill hurriedly exit R and as they do so, Dame Dobb enters L in a depressed state

Dame Oh, boys and girls. Everything's gone wrong since that spell got broken. There was a power cut in [local big store] this afternoon and for two hours, hundreds of shoppers were stranded on the escalators. And talk about trouble on the *trains*. The one from [nearby town] was four hours late when it arrived. "What kept you?" I said. "You should have been here ages ago." "I know", said the driver, "but we ran over [unpopular politician]". "Good heavens", I said, "What on earth was he doing on the railway lines?" "Oh", he said. "He wasn't on the lines ... but we got him all right."

Tommy dashes on L, looking flustered

Tommy (*to the audience*) Whatcha, kids. (*To Dame*) Ooooh. Quick, Pewty, quick. You've got to come back to the village. (*He attempts to pull her* L)

Dame (*resisting*) What for? So they can cut me head off and throw it in me face?

Tommy (*hastily*) No, no. You don't understand. Nobody's blaming *you*. It's Jack and Jill. They left a letter telling everybody what had happened, and then ran away.

Dame (*alarmed*) Oh, I say...

Tommy (*babbling*) And the *Fairy* came to tell us if they found the water and put it back in the well the spell would start working again, but nobody wanted *them* to go underground, so *Peter* said *he'd* find it and bring it back to Jack and Jill so *they* could tip it into the well again and stop the *Demon* from pinching everybody's happiness, but we don't know where Jack and Jill are and the Demon's gone down there first to try and stop him, leaving *imps* all over the village causing trouble, and as if *that* isn't bad enough, *I've* got a puncture in me mountain bike from looking for *you*. (*He gasps for air*)

Dame (*to the audience; drily*) You don't get storylines like this in [popular soap opera], do you? (*To Tommy*) What are you *talking* about, a puncture in your mountain bike? You've not come all this way on *that* rusty old thing.

Tommy 'Course I have. And it was murder pedalling up that last hill. Talk about *steep*. I'd have slid all the way to the bottom again if I hadn't kept my brakes on.

Dame (*after a reaction*) Never mind about *that*. The *first* thing that's got to be done is find Jack and Jill. Now... Has anybody called the police?

Tommy (*scornfully*) No. It's no use calling *them*. They're absolutely *useless*. Have you been in that police station lately? The walls are covered in pictures of criminals with "Wanted for Robbery", "Wanted for Forgery", and "Wanted for Murder" written underneath 'em in great big letters.

Dame Well, what's wrong with that?

Tommy (*patiently*) If they want 'em all *that* badly, why didn't they hold on to 'em when they were taking their photographs? (*Firmly*) No, no. If anybody's going to find 'em, we've got to do it ourselves. The Baron's offered a big reward, you know.

Dame (*surprised*) Oh, I say... (*Delightedly*) So if *we* find 'em, we'd have enough money to get married, wouldn't we? (*She beams at him*)

Tommy (*flustered*) Oh ... I ... er ... I don't know about *that*, Pewty. I mean... We hardly know each other. Besides ... When *I* get married, it's got to be to somebody as soft and gentle as a little turtle-dove.

Dame Well ... don't *I* remind you of a little turtle-dove? (*She simpers*)

Tommy (*aside*) Yes. You're pigeon-toed. (*Aloud*) No, no. Pewty. I couldn't marry *you*.

Dame Why not? You'd never have holes in your socks again.

Tommy (*brightening*) Wouldn't I?

Dame Course not. I'd teach you how to darn 'em.

Song 16: Dame and Tommy

At the end of the song Dame and Tommy exit R

Peter enters L, *carrying a small wooden pail*

Peter Just a few more minutes and I'll be climbing down the well. (*Apprehensively*) If only I knew what it's like down there ... *and* where to look for the spilled water. It all seemed so easy when I volunteered, but how do I tell the magic water from an ordinary pool? And if I don't find every drop of it ... whatever it looks like ... it'll all be a waste of time and we'll never get the spell working again. (*He shrugs*) Still... The sooner I'm underground, the more chance there'll be of finding it, bringing it back, and saying goodbye to Demon Discontent. Now where does that path begin?

Peter exits R

A moment later, Jack and Jill enter R

Jill (*excitedly*) Did you hear what Tommy said, Jack? If Peter finds the water
we spilled and *we* put it back in the well, the spell will start working again
and no-one will be cross with us.
Jack But what if he *doesn't* find it?
Jill (*firmly*) Of course he will ... if *we* help him.
Jack But that means *we'd* have to go down the well, too. And he'd never let
us do *that*.
Jill He couldn't stop us if we *followed* him. By the time he found out we were
there, it'd be much too late to send us back again.
Jack (*delightedly*) You're *right*. Then that's what we'll do.

Fetch enters L

Fetch (*spotting them*) Ooooooh. (*He calls* L) I've found 'em, I've found 'em.
Jill (*to Jack*) Quick. Quick.

Jack and Jill hurry off R *as Carry rushes on* L

Carry (*calling*) Here. Come back. (*To Fetch*) Get after 'em.

*Fetch and Carry set off in pursuit and a rapid fade brings the scene to an
end*

SCENE 3

The Land of Forgotten Toys

*The backdrop depicts a child's impression of blue skies with white, fluffy
clouds and rolling green hills sporting lollipop shaped trees. The façade of
an outsized wooden toy fort is* UR, *and an outsize Snakes and Ladders board
is* UL, *both masking entrances. The edge of a rocky cliff is* DR, *in which a cave
entrance is sited. Inside the cave can be glimpsed glistening rocky walls. An
outsize toy garage, farmhouse or similar is* DL

*When the scene begins, there is full Lighting and Antiquita, the Keeper of Past
Pleasures, stands* UC *supporting him/herself on a gnarled wooden staff. (NB:
The part can be played by a man or a woman—for the sake of expediency
Antiquita is henceforth referred to as male.) He is extremely old with long*

white hair, and (if played by a man) a matching long beard. He wears a faded and dusty-looking wizard's style cloak and pointed hat. In front of him, the stage is occupied by the Forgotten Toys: tin soldiers, soft toys, rag dolls, teddy bears, ballerinas, etc. of various periods and designs. Some look almost new, but others are ragged or patched, have stuffing poking out of them, or an eye, ear or limb missing. All are dancing

Dance 17: The Forgotten Toys

At the end of the dance, the toys cry out in surprise and fall back as Peter emerges from the cave R, *carrying the pail*

Peter (*amazed*) Where am I? (*He glances around*) What *is* this place?
Antiquita (*advancing slowly* DC) Greetings, young man. And welcome to our magical realm.
Peter (*drawing back*) Who are *you*?
Antiquita No need to be afraid. I am Antiquita, Keeper of Past Pleasures, and Guardian of all who live in the Land of Forgotten Toys. (*He indicates his surroundings*)
Peter (*awed*) But this is *amazing*. I never dreamed somewhere like this existed.
Antiquita (*chuckling*) That's hardly surprising. You're the first human ever to visit us ... though every one of these charming toys was once the favourite possession of *some* little girl or boy on earth.

The Toys nod their agreement

Peter (*gazing at them*) But ... but they're all *alive*.
Antiquita (*lightly*) Well, of course they are. Once I've rescued them from dusty attics and old cardboard boxes where they've lain for years, I bring them down here and give them a chance to enjoy themselves again. You've no *idea* how sad they become when their owners grow up and forget all about them. *Some* poor things just crumble into dust and vanish. (*He shakes his head in disbelief, then remembers himself*) But tell me... What brings *you* to our pleasant little land?
Peter I'm looking for the magic water that came from the well on top of our hill. Some of it soaked into the ground and came down here, and if I don't find it before Demon Discontent does, our kingdom's in terrible danger.

The Toys react

Antiquita (*realizing*) Ah... So that's what he's looking for. I *knew* he was up to something *sneaky* again. (*Confidentially*) We've been neighbours for years but none of the Toys like him. Far too nasty and self-satisfied. (*Reassuringly*) But don't worry. He hasn't found anything yet. Two of the Toys are watching his every move.

Peter (*relieved*) Then there's still a chance. But I have to hurry. Have you any idea where it *might* have fallen?

Antiquita I'm afraid not. But the rest of the toys will help. They'd love to see Discontent beaten for a change. Come. We'll begin the search at once.

Antiquita escorts Peter off L, *followed by the Toys*

Jack and Jill hurry on from the cave DR

Jack (*glancing over his shoulder*) Quick. Quick. They're right behind us.

Jill (*glancing round*) But where are we?

Jack I don't know, but we mustn't let them catch us. Let's hide again.

Jack and Jill hurry off DL *and vanish from view*

Fetch and Carry stagger on from the cave R *and come to a halt* C

Fetch (*gasping for air*) It's no use. We've lost 'em.

Carry (*annoyed*) Yes. And it's all *your* fault. You should have run faster.

Fetch (*protesting*) How could I? My legs are still hurting.

Carry Your legs? What's wrong with your legs?

Fetch I had to see the doctor this morning 'cause they were so swollen I could hardly get my trousers on.

Carry And did he tell you what was causing it?

Fetch No, but he gave me a prescription for a kilt.

Carry snatches off his hat and beats Fetch with it

Carry (*irately*) You're useless, you are. Absolutely useless. (*He puts his hat back on*) Well, that's it, then. We haven't a hope of getting that reward money, now. We may as well go back home to Arcady and get a job digging ditches.

Fetch You must be joking. I'm not doing *that* again. The last time I did it I was working with two fellers from [local town, or area] who never did a stroke. They just stood at the side of the hole with their shovels up in the air pretending to be street lamps while *I* did all the digging.

Carry Well, didn't you complain to the boss?

Fetch Course I did. So he gave 'em the sack and I had to look for another job.

Carry (*puzzled*) What for?

Fetch (*indignantly*) Well, I wasn't going to work in the *dark*, was I?

Carry (*after a reaction*) Look. I'll tell you what we'll do. Folks have been tossing coins into that well for donkey's years, haven't they? And they must have landed somewhere in *this* place. So let's have a quick look round and see if we can find some. We could end up with a fortune after all.
Fetch (*delightedly*) Oooooh. Good idea.

Fetch and Carry exit UR *eagerly scanning the ground*

The Lights dim and Demon appears L *in a green light*

Demon (*fuming*) A thousand curses. Not a trace of magic water found...
     And yet without a doubt, I know it's here beneath the ground.
     If Peter Pumpkin-eater should succeed where I have failed,
     My plans to rule the Earth collapse. I'm beaten. Foiled. Derailed.
     (*Smirking*) So just as a precaution, other plans I'll need to make,
     And then to win this game will be a simple piece of cake.

Demon laughs gleefully and exits DL

The green light goes out as Lights return to normal

Dame Dobb and Tommy emerge from the cave R

Tommy Whatcha, kids.

Audience response

Dame (*looking round in amazement*) Ooooh, I say...
Tommy (*nervously*) Where do you think we are, Pewty?
Dame I don't know, (*she sniffs the air*) but they definitely came this way. I can still smell the vinegar.
Tommy Well, I hope they've got a chemists down here. My throat's killing me. It's been sore ever since I swallowed one of the tree decorations last Christmas.
Dame I'm not surprised. You've probably got tinsil-itus. (*She chortles*)
Tommy Har har. Very funny. (*Plaintively*) But there must be something wrong with me. I'm starting to get all *cold* and *shivery*.
Dame (*concerned*) Perhaps you'd better go back and get an overcoat? They're ever so warm, you know. I saw a feller wearing one yesterday and *he* was *roasting*.
Tommy Was he?

Dame Oh, yes. I noticed as soon as he opened it up to show me the lining.

Tommy (*puzzled*) Show you the lining?

Dame (*reasonably*) What *else* could he have been showing me? He'd got nothing else on. (*She glances* DL) Oh, I say…

Tommy What? What?

Dame (*crossing him and moving* L) Look at this. (*She indicates a spot on the ground*)

Tommy (*following her*) What is it? (*He looks down at the same spot*)

Dame I dreamed about this last night. *This* (*she indicates the spot*) is the very spot where every time you sing a certain little song, you get a present.

Tommy (*startled*) Eh?

Dame It's true. Just one little song and the present's yours.

Tommy (*scoffing*) Give over.

Dame (*shrugging*) All right. Don't believe me. But watch this. (*She stands on the spot and sings*) Shure … a little bit of Heaven *fell…*

A large box of chocolates descends on a wire from above

(*After a slight pause*) …from out the sky one day…

The box halts beside her. She un-hooks the box and the wire is pulled up out of sight

(*Smugly*) See?

Dame opens the box and exits LC, *happily eating chocolates*

Tommy (*amazed*) Oooooh. Did you see that, kids? She got a big box of chocolates. (*Eagerly*) I'll have to have a go at that. (*He quickly positions himself*) Now how did that song go? (*He thinks quickly*) Oh, yes. (*He launches into song*) Shure … a little bit of Heaven *fell* … from out the sky one day.

On the word fell, *a large sack stuffed with rags or similar, drops from above him and hits him on the head. As he crashes to the floor, the sack is pulled up swiftly and vanishes from sight*

(*Staggering to his feet*) Oooooh. I don't know about a bit of *Heaven*. It felt more like a lump of *earth*. (*Indignantly*) I'm not doing *that* again. Let some other idiot do it. (*He rubs his head miserably*)

Fetch enters DL

Fetch What are *you* doing here? (*Suspiciously*) Are you *following* us?

Tommy Eh? (*He realizes*) Oh, no. No. (*He winks at the audience*) As a matter of fact I came down here to get my present.
Fetch Present? What present?
Tommy (*in mock surprise*) Didn't you know about it? I thought *everybody* knew about it. (*To the audience*) *You* know about it, don't you, kids?

Audience response

Fetch (*eagerly*) Well, tell me. Tell me.
Tommy All right. If you stand *here* ... on this very spot... (*he indicates it*) and sing "A little bit of Heaven" ... you get a big, big surprise.
Fetch (*eagerly*) What is it? What is it?
Tommy Oh, no no no. You have to sing the song first.
Fetch On that spot? (*He indicates it*)
Tommy On that spot.
Fetch Right.

With Tommy watching delightedly, Fetch positions himself and begins to sing. At the same point as before, the sack descends, knocks him flying and shoots back up out of sight

Tommy chortles and exits LC

Fetch staggers to his feet

Oooh, of all the rotten tricks. (*He rubs his head*)

Carry enters DL

Carry I might have known *you'd* be standing about doing nothing. You're dead idle, you are. And what are you rubbing your head for?
Fetch Oh ... well ... I was just thinking what I'd like for my present. (*He winks at the audience*)
Carry Present? *What* present?
Fetch The one you get when you stand on this spot here (*he indicates it*) and sing "A little bit of Heaven".
Carry "A little bit of Hea..." (*He pushes him*) Don't be so *stupid*. How can singing a silly little Irish song get you a present?
Fetch But it's true, (*to the audience*) isn't it, boys and girls?

Audience response

Carry (*glaring at them*) They're as daft as you are.
Fetch (*put out*) All right, then. All right. Just you try it and see.

Carry I *will*. (*Smugly*) Just to prove how barmy you all are. (*He positions himself and sings*)

At the same point as before, the sack drops down, knocks him flying and vanishes back out of sight

Fetch chortles and dashes out LC

Carry staggers to his feet

I'll flatten him. I'll flatten him. (*He clutches his head*)

Dame enters DL

Dame Oooh, I say ... you've not got a headache, have you?

Carry (*irately*) Of course I've got a headache. Wouldn't you have if a ten ton... (*Hastily*) Oh, no. No. As a matter of fact I was just thinking what sort of *present* I'd like.

Dame Present? Oh, I say. What a co-in-ci-dence. I like presents, as well. (*She beams*)

Carry (*heartily*) Do you? Well, in that case, I'll tell you a little secret. (*He simpers*)

Dame Oooh. I love secrets as well.

Carry (*beaming*) Did you know ... if you stand on this spot... (*He indicates it*) and sing "A little bit of Heaven" ... you get a big, big, big surprise?

Dame (*as if impressed*) You're *joking*. (*She beams at the audience*)

Carry I'm not. I'm *not*. It's absolutely guaranteed.

Dame "A little bit of Heaven". Well, I know that song. And you're quite sure that if I sing it I'll get a surprise?

Carry (*beaming*) Oh, yes. (*He winks at the audience and gives a "thumbs up" sign*)

Dame Well ... I'd better have a go, then. (*She positions herself and begins to sing, but as she reaches the word* fell, *she steps forward, arms outstretched*)

The sack falls behind her, so missing, and flies back up out of sight

Carry (*grabbing her arm*) No, no. You don't step *forward*. If you step forward, you won't get your surprise present. Didn't I tell you that?

Dame (*innocently*) No. No, you didn't. But not to worry. I'll sing it again, shall I? (*She positions herself again and begins to sing. At the same point, she steps backwards, arms outstretched and head thrown back*)

The sack falls in front of her, misses, and shoots back out of sight without her noticing it

Carry (*annoyed*) No, no, no, no, NO. (*He grabs her arm and pulls her forward*) You moved backwards, didn't you? You moved *backwards*. (*Patiently*) If you move *backwards*, you don't get your present.
Dame Oh, I see. But you didn't tell me that *before*, did you? You only said I mustn't move *forwards*.
Carry (*hastily*) I know. I know. It was *my* fault. I *should* have told you and I didn't but I'm telling you *now*. You don't step forwards and you don't step backwards. You stay stood standing *there*... (*He pushes her into position*) exactly where you are... and you don't move a muscle until you get your present. Understand?
Dame Yes. I'm sorry. I'll do it again. (*She begins to sing. At the same point she stops singing, steps sideways and taps him on the shoulder*)

The sack crashes down, misses her and shoots back up again

Will it be something heavy, this present? Because if it is, I don't know if I'll be able to carry it up that well by myself and——
Carry (*almost screaming with frustration*) Are you *stupid*? You did it again, didn't you? You moved out of the way. (*He tries to control himself*) I'll tell you one last time. You stand right here... (*He moves to the spot and stands*) You don't move forward... you don't move backward... you don't move sideways... you don't do a back somersault, jump in the air, ride a bicycle or eat fish and chips, you just stay right here and sing. (*He sings loudly*) "Shure a little bit of Heaven fell from out the sky one day".

The sack comes down and flattens him, then vanishes upwards

Dame Oh, I see... (*She stands on top of him and sings*)

At the usual point, a wicker basket comes down instead of the sack. Inside it is a large bottle of champagne. Dame removes this and the basket is drawn up

(*Displaying the bottle*) Thank you very much.

Dame exits DL happily, as Carry staggers to his feet and angrily chases after her

Peter and Antiquita enter UL, followed by the Toys. All look downhearted

Peter It's no use. We've searched everywhere. There's not a trace of the magic water.
Antiquita (*shaking his head*) And if it *did* come down here, the Toys couldn't help but find it. I'm afraid your journey's been in vain.

Tommy enters DL

Tommy No, it hasn't. Look who I've found.

Jack and Jill enter DL, *carrying a large gold watering can between them. Dame Dobb and Fetch and Carry follow*

Peter (*startled*) Jack. Jill. What are *you* doing here?

Jill (*hastily*) Spilling the water was all *our* fault, so we decided to follow you and help get it back in.

Jack And here it *is*. It'd dripped into this old watering can over there… (*he indicates off* L) and turned it into solid gold.

Toys and Antiquita react with astonishment

Peter (*delightedly*) Then all we have to do is replace it in the well before midnight and Discontent's well and truly beaten.

Everyone looks delighted

Jill (*hopefully*) Does this mean Uncle Barty won't be cross with us any more?

Peter (*tongue in cheek*) He may have *something* to say about keeping out of mischief in future, but in view of all the help you've been, I think he'll be only too happy to let bygones be bygones.

All smile happily

And as for *me*… Well … all *I* want to do is get back to Muddlethrough Manor and ask his permission to marry Marjory. And if he does say yes … then with her beside me, I'll be the happiest man in all Arcadia.

Song 18: Peter and Ensemble

At the end of the song, Baron hurries on from the cave R

Baron (*panting*) Oh, my goodness. Quick. Quick. It's Demon Discontent. He's kidnapped Marjory.

Everyone reacts with dismay and the Lights fade rapidly to end the scene

SCENE 4

On the way to the Demon's Lair

A lane scene depicting gnarled and eerie looking trees. Half lighting

Demon enters L and beckons R

Marjory enters R, pulled by two small imps

Marjory (*struggling*) Let go of me. Let go.
Demon (*triumphantly*) In vain you plead. Until the hour all Earth is in my
        sway
        And Fairy Rainbow's beaten ... in my Kingdom you shall
        stay.
Marjory (*defiantly*) That's what *you* think. When Peter finds out what's
happened, this is the *first* place he'll come to look for me.
Demon   Of course it is. And that, my dear's exactly what I've planned.
        A spratt to catch a mackerel is the ploy, you understand.
        For if the magic water ... by that Pumpkin-eating brat...
        Is somehow found, I'll swap you ... very willingly ... for *that*;
        Which means ... it never will be to the ancient Well returned
        And proves that even fairy folk can get their fingers burned.
        (*He chuckles*)
        But now we must away, for yonder lies my demon lair, (*he
        indicates L*)
        Where till he comes in search of you, my company you'll
        share...

Demon signals to the imps and exits L

Struggling and protesting, Marjory is dragged off after him

The Fairy enters R in a white follow spot

Fairy   Once more he's over-confident. Of that there is no doubt.
        For demon schemes are sure to fail when fairy magic is about
        Despite his boastful claims, I vow he'll end this day dejected
        When retribution seeks him out in manner unexpected.
        So to his baleful dwelling place, young Peter I will lead,
        And put an end to misery, misfortune, crime and greed.

Fairy exits R

Tommy enters L

Tommy Whatcha, kids.

Audience response

Here. You've not seen the others anywhere, have you? We all went different ways looking for Marjory, but I've managed to lose myself and I don't like it round here. (*He glances around uneasily*) It's all creepy and horrible.

Dame hurriedly enters R *in a new creation*

Dame (*panting*) Oh, I say... Thank goodness I've found you. I don't like being on my own in places like this. It reminds me of [local area]. You won't catch me going *there* again.
Tommy (*curiously*) Why? What's wrong with it?
Dame I was walking down there last week when *suddenly* a strange feller jumped out in front of me and told me to hand over all me money. "But I haven't got any," I told him. "Not a *penny.*"
Tommy (*horrified*) And what did he say?
Dame He said he didn't believe me ... and if I didn't hand some cash over right away, he was going to *search me himself.*
Tommy (*scornfully*) He wouldn't have *dared.*
Dame But he did. He *did*. He searched me from top to toe. All over. Every inch and centipede.
Tommy (*aghast*) And did he find anything?
Dame No. But I enjoyed it so much, I gave him my credit card. (*She chortles*)
Tommy (*put out*) Oh, there you go again. Telling fibs to make me jealous. Well, I don't want to know. Where's everybody else got to?
Dame Don't ask me. I haven't seen 'em in ages. (*She glances off* R) But here comes the Baron.

Baron enters R

Where's Jack and Jill?
Baron They've persuaded Fetch and Carry to take them for a swim in that little lake while we rescue Marjory from that horrible Demon. Then as soon as that's done, perhaps we can join them?
Tommy (*hastily*) Oh, no. Not me. I've not been swimming since I was five years old and got banned from the [local swimming centre].
Dame (*surprised*) What for?
Tommy (*embarrassed*) Doing a wee-wee in the water.

Baron (*amused*) But every little boy does *that*, Thomas.

Tommy Yes. But not from the top diving board.

Baron (*hastily*) Oh ... well ... er ... perhaps we'd better get on with the search? (*He glances round worriedly*) There's something very *odd* about this place. It's too dark and dismal. It wouldn't surprise me if it were haunted.

Dame (*pushing him playfully*) Don't be silly. There's no such things as ghosts.

Tommy There *is*. One of 'em floated in through the [local cafe]'s wall last week and the manager had to chuck it out.

Baron Why was that?

Tommy It wanted a double brandy and they don't serve spirits.

Dame (*primly*) Well, ghosts don't scare *me*.

Baron (*impressed*) Haven't you *ever* been scared, Putrescence?

Dame (*firmly*) Never. (*She reconsiders*) Well ... maybe *once*, I have. I crossed a fully-grown sheepdog with a blackcurrant jelly.

Tommy (*incredulously*) And that scared you?

Dame Of course it did. It gave me the colly-wobbles. I was so *scared*, the doctor told me I'd only five minutes left to live. *Five minutes*. "You must be joking", I said. "Surely you can do something for me?" "Well", he said, "There is *one* thing".

Baron (*all agog*) And what *was* it?

Dame He offered to boil me an egg.

Tommy (*impatiently*) Ohhhh, come on. Let's go find Marjory. (*He prepares to exit* L)

Baron (*hastily*) Just a minute. Just a minute. What if there's something nasty, repulsive and horrible about?

Dame (*dismissively*) Oh ... there won't be a Local/General Election for ages.

Tommy No. No. He's right. We ought to have somebody to *warn* us. (*Brightly*) I know... We'll ask all my pals in the audience. (*To the audience*) Did you hear that, kids? If you see anything creepy and crawly following us, just yell out at the top of your voices so we'll know it's there and we can get away. Will you do that?

Audience response

Baron (*relieved*) Oh, that's marvellous. And you won't forget, will you?

Audience response

Dame Well, we can make sure of *that*, can't we? We'll have a *rehearse* with 'em. Suppose we stand here and sing a little song, or something, as though we haven't a care in the world ... then *they* can pretend they've *seen* something and shout as loud as they can so we'll know there's something there that's not supposed to be.

Tommy What a good idea. What shall we sing?

They decide on a song

Right. Off we go then. *We* start to sing. *They* pretend there's something behind us, and *we* get a warning. (*Happily*) Can't go wrong.

They begin to sing

A Ghost enters L, *drifts behind them and as the audience respond, exits* R

The trio stop singing

Dame (*pleased*) Oh, that was good, wasn't it? *Very* good.

Baron (*beaming*) Yes. The little girl down there (*he indicates*) was shouting so loud, I nearly believed there *was* something there. (*He chuckles*) Didn't you, Thomas?

Tommy Well ... it was all *right*. But that miserable feller over there (*he indicates vaguely*) never opened his mouth. I think we should try it again.

They begin to sing again

The Ghost enters R, *drifts behind them and exits* L, *as the audience responds*

The trio stop singing

Dame Well, that was a *lot* better. It even woke Mrs [local well-known person] up.

Baron (*peering into the audience*) Which one is *she*?

Dame Oh, she's not *here*. She's on holiday in Majorca.

Tommy (*doubtfully*) I still think they could shout *louder*. Let's have one more try. And this time see if you can bring the roof down.

They begin singing again

The Ghost enters L, *glides behind them and remains*

As the audience responds, the trio stop singing

That's smashing. That's just the volume we need.

Baron and Dame agree

So remember, boys and girls. If you see something scary, that's the ... that's the ... that's the... (*He attempts vainly to calm them*) No, no. You can stop shouting now. You only have to do it if you *see* something. (*To the others*) I can't understand it. They won't stop.
Dame (*uneasily*) No. And *I* know why. They're saying there's a ghost *behind* us.
Tommy (*uncertainly*) They're having us on. (*To the audience*) Aren't you?
Baron Well, I think we'd better have a look. Just to make sure.
Dame All right, then. We'll count up to three, then we'll all turn round and if there is a ghost ... we'll grab it.
Tommy Good idea.

They begin to count. As they do so, the Ghost ducks down and when they spin round, look over its head. Seeing nothing, they turn back. As they do so, the Ghost stands up again

Baron Nothing there at all.
Dame (*smugly*) I knew it all the time. (*She wags her finger at the audience*) Little rascals. You're worse than Jack and Jill, you are.
Tommy (*uneasily*) I don't know, Pewty ... they seem very sure. Perhaps we should have a look round?
Dame Oh, all right, then. If it'll make you happy. Let's go that way. (*She indicates* L)

The Ghost moves to the end of the line R, and to the accompaniment of creepy music they tiptoe L, and execute a circle, ending in their original positions

Baron Not a sausage.
Tommy (*not happy*) They're still shouting, though. Maybe we should look the other way?
Dame Ooooh, you're never satisfied, are you? All right. We'll go the other way.

The Ghost moves to the end of line L, and the business is repeated as before

There you are. Nothing at all. Now let's get on with it and finish the song.

They begin singing again. The Ghost taps Tommy on the shoulder

Tommy turns his head, sees the Ghost, screams and runs off L, followed by the Ghost

The others stop singing and notice Tommy is missing

Baron (*puzzled*) Where's Thomas?
Dame (*thinking*) It must be his move. He's playing chess with his pet dog.
Baron Playing chess? (*Impressed*) It must be a very clever dog.
Dame Not really. It's only beaten him twice.

They begin to sing again

The Ghost enters and taps Baron on the shoulder

Baron turns, screams and exits R, chased by Ghost

Dame stops singing

(*Scared*) Barty? Oooh, I say. Where's he gone? He's left me on my own.
There's nobody here but me. (*To the audience*) It wasn't a ghost, was it?

Audience response

Ooo-er. I wonder if it'll go away if I sing loudly? 'Cos they don't like loud
singing, ghosts don't and I've got a really loud voice. You should have
heard it last night. The manager told me it *filled* this place. Well ... it must
have done, 'cos I noticed a lot of the audience left to make room for it. (*She
takes a deep breath*) Oh, well ... here goes. (*She begins to sing*)

The Ghost enters and taps her on the shoulder

She turns, the Ghost screams in terror and exits

Dame watches it go, then turns to the audience

(*Disgustedly*) Music critics.

Dame follows the Ghost off and the Lights rapidly fade to a Black-out

SCENE 5

Inside the Demon's Lair

*A gloomy-looking castle interior. Huge stone pillars mask entrances and
exits L and R. A large throne made of roughly hewn stone is atop a rocky-
looking daïs and is placed UL, slightly in front of the rear pillar. Huge
candelabra provide pools of light to partially illuminate the room*

When the scene begins, a family of Rats are dancing a lively tarantella

Dance 19: Rats

At the end of the dance, Marjory enters UL, *from behind the throne, causing the Rats to squeal in fright and rapidly exit*

Looking around the room in dismay, Marjory moves DC

Marjory What a horrible place. So cold and gloomy. (*Firmly*) But I'd stay here *forever* rather than let that horrible demon get hold of the Magic Well water. (*She sighs*) Oh, if only I knew where Peter is so I could warn him. (*Sadly*) But I don't even know where *I* am. All I *do* know is that somewhere out there he's looking for me and he'll never give up till we're together again.

Song 20: Marjory (Optional)

At the end of the song, Peter enters UR

Peter Marjory. (*He hurries down to her*)
Marjory (*delightedly*) Peter. (*She hugs him*) How did you find me?
Peter (*hastily*) I'll explain later. But first we must get back to Arcady and replace the magic water in the well. Another hour and it'll be too late.
Marjory (*worriedly*) But how can we *do* that? There's no way out of here.
Peter (*amused*) Of course there is. We'll leave the same way I came *in*. Through the door over there. (*He indicates* R)
Marjory (*shaking her head*) You don't understand. The Demon's put a *spell* on the castle. Anyone can come *in*, but without his permission, they can't get *out* again. That's why he doesn't need guards.
Peter (*stunned*) There must be *some* way. (*Firmly*) Come on. We'll try over there.

Taking her hand, Peter leads Marjory UL *and they hastily exit*

Fetch and Carry enter UR *and apprehensively move* DC

Fetch (*glancing round*) So *this* is [local council offices].

Carry snatches his hat off and beats Fetch across the shoulder with it

(*Pained*) Ow. Ow. Ow. (*He rubs his shoulder*)
Carry (*pulling his hat back on*) We'll have less of the levity, if you *don't* mind. Thanks to you, we're in an even *worse* mess than we were *before*.

How could you let Jack and Jill get away from you again? You were supposed to be teaching them to swim while I had forty winks.

Fetch (*protesting*) I was. I was. But they wanted to know how fast *I* could swim, so I jumped into the lake and showed 'em. (*Proudly*) I'd have got a gold medal at the Olympic Games for a swim like that. Two hundred metres in three seconds flat.

Carry (*scornfully*) Don't be *ridiculous*. How could you swim two hundred metres in three seconds flat?

Fetch I went over a waterfall. By the time I got out again, they'd hopped it.

Carry (*disgustedly*) And now look where you've landed us. In a ruined castle ... miles from anywhere. We'll need a *plane* to get back from here.

Fetch (*alarmed*) You're not getting *me* in a plane again. The last time I went up in one of them things, it ran out of petrol half-way across the Atlantic.

Carry And did it crash?

Fetch No. But all the passengers had to get out and push.

Carry snatches off his hat and slaps Fetch with it

Tommy enters R

Tommy Whatcha, kids. (*He notices Fetch and Carry*) What are *you* doing here?

Carry (*hastily*) Never mind us. Where's Dame Dobb?

Tommy Outside in the garden. She was just coming up the steps when she tripped, fell over the balustrade, laddered her new tights and rolled into a muddy ditch.

Fetch Oooh, I bet that made her mad. What did she say?

Tommy Leaving out the *naughty* words?

Carry (*shocked*) I should hope so.

Tommy Well, in that case she didn't say anything.

Dame enters R, in a grotesque new outfit, carrying a thermos flask

Dame (*beaming*) Yoo-hoo. Ooooh, I say ... You'll never guess what? I think old Antiquita's taken a fancy to me. Look what he's given me. (*She shows the flask*)

Tommy What is it?

Dame It's a Thermos flask. (*She displays it once again*)

Fetch (*puzzled*) And what does it do?

Dame What do you mean, "What does it *do*"? (*Patiently*) If you put *hot* things in it, it keeps 'em hot ... and if you put *cold* things in it, it keeps 'em cold.

Carry And what have *you* put in it?

Dame Two cups of coffee and six choc ices. (*She glances round*) Where's Jack and Jill?

Fetch (*hastily*) Oh. They ... er ... they've gone off to hide. We're playing Hide and Seek, you see?

Tommy (*brightening*) Oh, I like Hide and Seek, don't you, Pewty?

Dame Well ... *yes*. But I'd sooner play Jockey's Knock.

Carry (*puzzled*) What's Jockey's Knock?

Dame It's the same as Postman's Knock ... but there's a lot more horseplay. (*She chortles*)

Baron enters R, looking worried

Baron Has anyone found Marjory, yet? We *must* get back to Arcady and it's almost midnight.

Tommy Midnight? (*He yawns*) No wonder I'm tired, then. I spent all last night looking at the bedroom ceiling.

Fetch What for?

Tommy I've got insomnia.

Dame Well, that's your own fault. You should get more sleep.

Peter and Marjory hurry in DL

Baron (*spotting them*) Marjory.

Marjory (*surprised*) Uncle Barty. Everybody.

Peter (*groaning*) Oh, no. Now we're *all* trapped.

Demon enters UL, holding a large iron key

All react

Demon (*smirking*) Indeed you are. And as my slaves, *forever*, here you'll stay.

Earth's happiness has filled my flask; I've stolen ev'ry scrap away.

Now safe from prying fairy eyes, I vow 'twill ever be

In cupboard locked securely. Yes. And *mine* the only key. (*He displays it and laughs harshly*)

Peter (*defiantly*) You haven't won, yet, Discontent. It's not quite midnight, and Jack and Jill still have the Magic Water.

Demon (*smirking*) I quite agee. Without a doubt the claim you make is true. (*He sits*)

But don't, I pray, build up your hopes. (*He grins*) I have the children too.

All react with dismay as Jack and Jill enter UL, carrying the golden watering can. They halt at the side of the throne

Tommy (*defeatedly*) Well, that's it then. We're done for.
Baron Oh, what's it matter as long as they're safe? (*To Jack and Jill*) Come and give your dear old Uncle a great big hug. (*He extends his arms to them*)
Jack (*primly*) No, thank you. We've got a *new* Uncle, now.

Everyone looks surprised

Jill (*haughtily*) And *he's* going to let us do whatever we *want* to do. Not go to stupid *school* and *learn* things.
Jack We can watch television *all day* if we like. *And* surf the Internet or play video games.
Dame (*incredulously*) Who *is* he? The Head of Social Services?
Jill (*pertly*) It's Uncle Discontent, of course.

She smiles sweetly at the triumphant Demon as everyone watches aghast

Demon (*smugly*) Now all that's left for me to do
Is take that water clear (*He indicates the watering can*)
And in a bottle keep it
As a charming souvenir.
Jack (*putting the watering can down*) *We* can do *that* for you, Uncle Discontent.
Demon (*smiling*) Of course you can. Then hasten. (*He gives the key to Jack*)
Bring a bottle from the shelf. (*He hesitates*)
Though just for satisfaction, I may fill it up myself. (*He chuckles*)

Jack and Jill exit L

Fetch (*disgustedly*) Well, the little ferrets.
Carry After all we've done for 'em.
Baron (*brokenly*) I don't believe it.
Dame (*soothingly*) Oh, don't get upset. This could be just like that story in the Bible. You know ... the one where the prodigal son ran away from home, but then felt sorry about it and came back again and made everybody happy.
Tommy (*interrupting*) Not *everybody*, Pewty.
Dame (*surprised*) What do you mean, "not everybody"? Who wasn't happy when the prodigal son came home?
Tommy The fatted calf.

Marjory (*to Peter*) Oh, Peter. What are we going to do?
Peter (*bravely*) Don't worry, Marjory. I'll think of *something*. But if ever I get my hands on those little monsters...

Jack and Jill enter L. *Jack carries an empty duplicate of the "Happiness" bottle*

Jack (*handing the bottle to Demon*) Here you are, *Uncle*.
Demon   I thank you. Now, the final task... (*He recognizes it and stares in horror*)
Oh, no. (*Almost speechless*) It cannot *be*.
This bottle held the "happiness"...
Its label I can see. (*He staggers to his feet*)
I locked it in my *cupboard* ... with the stopper firmly *on*...
But now the seal is *broken* and all trace of it has *gone*. (*He clutches his head*)

Others look at him in surprise

Jill (*innocently*) Well ... you *did* say you wanted a bottle to put the water in, so we emptied *that* one.
Jack (*innocently*) Though why you want a bottle of *pond* water for a souvenir, we can't imagine.

Everyone reacts in surprise

Baron (*blinking*) Pond water?
Jack Oh, yes. We put the *magic* water back in the well *ages* ago ... just as the Fairy told us to.

Everyone reacts

Tommy (*baffled*) Then what was all that "New Uncle" thing about?
Jill That was *her* idea. She knew Mr Discontent never kept his promises, so she told us how we could get our own back for the nasty trick he played on us. (*To Demon*) And that's exactly what we've done. (*She pulls a face at him*)

Everyone laughs with delight but Discontent

Peter Then the spell's *working* again? And everything's back to normal?

Fairy enters R

Fairy   Just so. And thanks to Jack and Jill, all merriment and mirth
                   Is even now returning to its rightful place on Earth.
Demon (*snarling*) But not for good. Although a thousand years it takes to
                   do it…
                   I'll gather ev'ry scrap again.
Fetch (*scornfully*) Go soak your head.
Carry   And *stew* it.

Demon lets out a howl of rage and exits L *carrying the bottle as all the
mortals celebrate*

Fairy (*amused*) Poor Discontent. For centuries he's plagued the human race,
                   But from now on, in Arcady, he'll nevermore dare show his
                   face
                   So back there, via the Magic Well, it's time to make your way,
                   That steeple bells may shortly ring to celebrate a *special* day.
                   For if the Baron deems it so, and I suspect he *will*…
                   A wedding chime will end this merry tale of Jack and Jill.
Dame (*simpering*) Ooh, you little saucepot. He's not even proposed to me
yet.

She throws an amorous glance at Tommy who cringes

Fairy (*smiling*) Step forward, Master Peter. Ask your question loud and
                   clear.
                   So all can hear the answer that you long so much to hear.
Peter (*stepping forward nervously and speaking to Baron*) I know I'm only
                   a gardener, sir, but … may I ask for Marjory's hand in marriage?
Marjory (*hurrying forward*) Please, Uncle Barty.
Jack ⎤ (*together*) Please.
Jill ⎦

There is a long pause as Baron pretends to think

Baron (*delightedly*) Of *course* you may. And we'll make quite sure that *this*
years's Betrothal Ball will be the biggest one Arcadia's ever seen.

Everyone cheers delightedly

*As Antiquita and the Toys crowd into the castle the whole company burst
into a joyful song*

Song 21: Company

At the end of the song there is general celebration as the Lights fade and the scene ends

SCENE 6

A Corridor in Muddlethrough Manor

A lane scene. Full Lighting

Tommy enters

Tommy Whatcha, kids.

Audience response

Well, here we are. Back in Arcadia. Getting ready for the wedding. And they're all coming to it, you know. All the famous folks. There's film stars, pop singers, football players. Oh, and there's one local councilor. Mind you ... he's invited himself because he wants to ask folks for money to put a king-sized statue of [Prime Minister] outside the Town Hall. It's a *smashing* idea, isn't it? Just what this place needs. It'll give shelter when it's raining, shade when it's hot and a chance for the pigeons to speak for all of us. There is *one* problem, though. Half the church choir's gone on holiday, so we haven't got many singers. But *I've* had a thought. Oh. Yes. If we invite everybody in the audience to come along as well, you could all help out with the singing. Would you like that? Right. Well, I'll tell you what we'll do. I've asked [selected cast member(s)] to write all the words down on a great big board so you can all read 'em ... and we'll have a little practice to see how good you are.

He calls on his assistant(s) and with whatever ad libbing is necessary they conduct the Song Sheet

As the song is sung for the last time, the assistant(s) exit, leaving Tommy to end it

Song 22: Company (Reprise)

At the end of the song, Tommy exits as the Lights fade rapidly to a Blackout

SCENE 7

The Ballroom and Finale

Full set. A spectacular Ballroom. Full Lighting

When the scene begins, Dancers in their finale costumes are dancing to the Walk-down music selected

Following a 36 bar routine, they exit L *and* R *as the Walk-down commences in the following order*

> *Chorus Members*
> *Dancers*
> *Antiquita*
> *Demelzia and Tonio*
> *The Rainbow Fairy*
> *Demon Discontent*
> *Baron Bumble*
> *Fetch and Carry*
> *Jack and Jill*
> *Dame Dobb*
> *Tommy*
> *Peter and Marjory*

When all are in their final positions, the music stops and Peter steps forward for the first line of the couplets

Peter   Our pantomime is ended. It's time to say good-night.
Marjory   We hope our entertainment brought you moments of delight.
Tommy   And in the years that have to come, you'll all remember still,
Dame   The happy time you spent with us and the tale of,
All   Jack and Jill.

There is a reprise of the Walk-down music which is now sung by the entire company, at the end of which——

——the CURTAIN *falls*

FURNITURE AND PROPERTY LIST

Further dressing may be added at the director's discretion

ACT I

PROLOGUE

On stage: Demon's bulbous bottle almost full of bright yellow liquid, stoppered by large cork, labelled "Essence of Happiness"

Off stage: Crystal ball on velvet cushion (**Imp**)

Personal: **Fairy:** wand

SCENE 1

Off stage: Bulbous bottle of liquid (**Demon**)
Large mobile phone on large wheels attached to long cord (**Tommy**)

Personal: **Fetch:** hat (throughout)
Carry: hat (throughout)

SCENE 2

Off stage: Bulbous bottle of liquid (**Demon**)
Battered old hat (**Carry**)

Personal: **Fetch:** ten pound note
Tommy: 2 ten pound notes
Carry: ten pound note

SCENE 3

On stage: High wall with central arch
Small pumpkin plants
Blossom-laden trees
Garden shed with practical door

Water butt
Watering cans
Plant pots

Off stage: Small plates holding slices of currant cake (**Jack** and **Jill**)
Watering can (**Peter**)

SCENE 4

Off stage: Pails (**Peter** and **Villagers**)
2 buckets (**Tommy**)
Small pail with rope handle (**Jack** and **Jill**)

SCENE 5

On stage: Magic well as described on page 27
Large rocks
Bushes
Floral garlands
Clothes-pegs

Off stage: Pail (**Jack** and **Jill**)
Pail (**Jack**)
Bulbous bottle of liquid (**Demon**)

Personal: **Crone:** playing cards

ACT II

SCENE 1

On stage: Suits of armour
Ancestral portraits
Feather dusters
Silver trays

Off stage: Large plate (**Tommy**)
Bulbous bottle of liquid (**Demon**)

Personal: **Jack:** wet-looking brown paper
Tommy: handkerchief

Scene 2

Off stage: Small fardel on stick (**Jack**)
Fardel on stick (**Jill**)
Small wooden pail (**Peter**)

Scene 3

On stage: Façade of outsized wooden toy fort
Outsize Snakes and Ladders board
Edge of rocky cliff
Outsize toy garage, farmhouse or similar
Forgotten Toys: tin soldiers, soft toys, rag dolls, teddy bears,
      ballerinas

Off stage: Pail (**Peter**)
Box of chocolates on wire (**SM**)
Large sack stuffed with rags or similar on wire (**SM**)
Wicker basket containing large bottle of champagne (**SM**)
Large gold watering can (**Jack** and **Jill**)

Scene 4

On stage: Lane scene

Scene 5

On stage: Huge stone pillars
Large throne made of roughly hewn stone atop rocky-looking dais
Huge lit candelabra

Off stage: Thermos flask (**Dame**)
Large iron key (**Demon**)
Golden watering can (**Jack** and **Jill**)
Empty duplicate of **Demon**'s bottle (**Jack**)

Scene 6

On stage: Stately home corridor fittings

Scene 7

On stage: Ballroom fittings

LIGHTING PLOT

Property fittings required: candelabra
Various interior and exterior settings

ACT I, Prologue

To open: Green follow spot on **Demon**

Cue 1   **Rainbow Fairy** enters   (Page 2)
             White follow spot on **Fairy**

Cue 2   **Fairy** waves her wand   (Page 3)
             Instant black-out

ACT I, Scene 1

To open: Overall general lighting

Cue 3   **Jack** and **Jill** exit   (Page 8)
             Dim lights and bring up green follow spot on **Demon**
                when he appears

Cue 4   **Demon** rocks with laughter   (Page 8)
             Bring up general lighting, fade out spot

Cue 5   At end of song all begin to exit   (Page 13)
             Fade lights to black-out

ACT I, Scene 2

To open: Dim general lighting

Cue 6   **Demon** enters   (Page 13)
             Bring up green follow spot on **Demon**

Cue 7	**Fairy** enters *Bring up white follow spot on* **Fairy**	(Page 13)
Cue 8	**Demon** exits *Cut green spot*	(Page 14)
Cue 9	**Fairy** exits *Return lights to full*	(Page 14)
Cue 10	**Fetch** and **Carry** exit *Rapidly fade to black-out*	(Page 17)

ACT I, Scene 3

To open: Full lighting

Cue 11	**Peter** and **Marjory** exit *Dim lights*	(Page 20)
Cue 12	**Demon** enters *Bring up green spot*	(Page 20)
Cue 13	**Fairy** enters *Bring up white follow spot on* **Fairy**	(Page 20)
Cue 14	**Fairy** exits *Cut follow spot*	(Page 21)
Cue 15	**Demon** exits *Cut green follow spot and return lights to normal*	(Page 21)
Cue 16	At end of song, **All** exit *Rapidly fade lights*	(Page 22)

ACT I, Scene 4

To open: Full lighting

Cue 17	**Demon** enters *Green follow spot on* **Demon**	(Page 25)

Cue 18   **Demon** exits   (Page 26)
              Rapidly fade lights to black-out

ACT I, SCENE 5

To open: Overall general lighting

Cue 19   **Demelzia**: "...I may just know one you will like."   (Page 28)
              Dim lights

Cue 20   At end of song   (Page 28)
              Return lights to normal

Cue 21   **Carry**: "It's too late."   (Page 32)
              Rapidly dim lights, flash, then bring up green follow spot
                on **Demon** *who enters*

ACT II, SCENE 1

To open: Overall general lighting

Cue 22   **Peter**: "...we want to ask you."   (Page 39)
              Flash, then dim lights and bring up green follow spot
                on **Demon** *who enters*

Cue 23   **Fairy** enters   (Page 39)
              Bring up white follow spot on **Fairy**

Cue 24   **Fairy** exits   (Page 40)
              Cut white follow spot

Cue 25   **Demon** rapidly exits   (Page 41)
              Cut green light and restore normal level

Cue 26   At end of song   (Page 41)
              Black-out

ACT II, SCENE 2

To open: Full lighting

Cue 27   **Fetch** and **Carry** exit   (Page 44)
             Rapidly fade lights

ACT II, Scene 3

To open: Full lighting

Cue 28   **Fetch** and **Carry** exit   (Page 47)
             Dim lights and bring up green spot on **Demon** *who enters*

Cue 29   **Demon** exits   (Page 47)
             Cut green light and return lights to normal

Cue 30   Everyone reacts with dismay   (Page 52)
             Rapidly fade lights

ACT II, Scene 4

To open: Half lighting

Cue 31   **Rainbow Fairy** enters   (Page 53)
             Bring up white follow spot on **Fairy**

Cue 32   **Dame** follows **Ghost** off   (Page 58)
             Rapidly fade lights to black-out

ACT II, Scene 5

To open: Gloomy lighting with candelabra

Cue 33   At end of song   (Page 65)
             Fade lights

ACT II, Scene 6

To open: Full lighting

Cue 34   At end of song, **Tommy** exits   (Page 65)
             Rapidly fade lights to black-out

ACT II, SCENE 7

To open: Full lighting

No cues

EFFECTS PLOT

ACT I

Cue 1   **Jack** indicates pail   (Page 25)
Flash

Cue 2   Lights dim rapidly   (Page 32)
Flash

ACT II

Cue 3   **Peter**: "…important we want to ask you."   (Page 39)
Flash

MADE AND PRINTED IN GREAT BRITAIN BY
LATIMER TREND & COMPANY LTD PLYMOUTH
MADE IN ENGLAND